CW00862930

O

BULLDOG SPIRIT!

COURAGE, HUMOUR, LOVE

V.J.ULLIOTT

Locket Press

Warwickshire

Cover Illustration via:

http//thebookcoverdesigner.com/designerbetibup33

Published by: Locket Press,Warwickshire:

locketpress@gmail.com

Our...Bulldog Spirit! Copyright © 2015 by V.J.Ulliott.

ABOUT THE BOOK

'Our...Bulldog Spirit' is a biographical novel based on the memories of my extended family.

Starting with the worst night of the Coventry blitz, 14 November 1940. Baby Shirley lay on the floor under the house stairs with her terrified family; Three year old Roy watched, clinging to his family in a frosty field six miles away.

The story follows their lives as they face tragedy and austerity with inspirational courage and humour.

Their love of life results in hilarious misadventures whilst:

Swimming in canals and rivers; riding bareback; befriending gypsies and boat people; joining in cycle rallies on the bombsites; singing with German POW's;

MAY YOUR FEARS

GIVE YOU STRENGTH!

rabbiting and boxing.

It is interwoven throughout and culminates in a beautiful, moving love story of timeless appeal.

***

Whilst events, places and people are real some names have been altered. Some events may not be in the precise order that they happened because memory is like that....Think of a vivid event from your school days...can you remember exactly when? For the flow of the novel and in the spirit of the book, I have also had to improvise on a few conversations, using my knowledge of the people to write what they probably would have said. But I must stress that even many of the conversations in this book are from vivid, true recollections, possibly so vivid because of the intensity of the events.

Some of the recollections seemed too remarkable or odd to be true, for example; my father not having his name on his birth certificate. After many hours of doubt and research, I found that it was, like everything that he and others described, both remarkable and true.

It has been an honour and a privilege to re-tell this wonderful story.

V.J.Ulliott (The Listener)

This book is dedicated to my family, past, present and future and to.......

Bulldogs....everywhere!

(People battling on against the odds to improve life.)

CHAPTERS.

Chapter 1

MOONLIGHT SONATA.

It was a Thursday afternoon... 14th November 1940. Looking in the mirror, Alice Thompson removed the curlers from her black hair and brushed it into place, then she took off the flowery pinny that she wore all day to protect her clothes. She liked to look nice for her husband, Wally, coming home from work. Her face was the finishing touch.

She had got her home immaculate. She was very proud of it; especially the parlour which she kept for best for her husband and special visitors. She had fed herself and the girls; Betty 8 years old, with black hair and twinkly blue eyes, little Jean 4 years old and very similar to Betty and dressed identically, then baby Shirley just 8 months old with soft gingerish baby curls. Wally's dinner was in the oven so that she could put it on the table immediately he entered the door.

'Keep the noise down please, your father'll be here any minute,' she called.

The girls didn't really need telling; there was a clock on the mantelpiece and they knew the unchangeable routine. Alice just had time to put a bit of red lipstick on before the front door opened.

Walter, mostly called 'Wally' was glad to be home after a long shift in a munitions factory and he had some chirpy news:

'We've been invited to a party down at the local tonight, in the pub cellar. It should be a good do. The girls are invited as well, it's a family do.'

Home-loving Alice always looked for excuses not to go out. She didn't even leave her home when the air raid sirens sounded. The air raid shelters were crammed full of people she didn't know with very few makeshift toilets. She couldn't face them even though they lived in quite a high risk area in the centre of Coventry, George Street, just a few streets away from the magnificent cathedral, in an area where houses were interwoven with munitions factories that not long

11

before had manufactured cars, bikes and watches for world leading companies. Luckily they hadn't had the trouble that they had been warned of and it was much more comfortable to stay at home, especially now that it was getting cold. Tonight though, she really had an excuse not to party:

'Oh Wally I really can't; there's an old lady down the end of the street on her own and she's really frightened with all this war talk. I promised I'd go and sit with her tonight, I can't let her down.'

Wally wasn't surprised, he normally went without her; she was kind and friendly to people but very shy when it came to social events or anything new.

'Well I'm going. I'm not letting my mates down.'

He worked long shifts and was an ARP warden. This meant staying up all night some nights on air raid patrol, after working in the factory all day, then going to work the following morning for another long shift. He wished she'd come but HE wasn't missing a party.

After washing up Wally's dinner plate and helping him get ready Alice set off with the children. It was a frosty November night. Winter had arrived early. The area was in a bit of a dip which made it foggy most of the time, but tonight it was crystal clear with a bright, clear, full moon. Alice thought it was winking at them. It was so pretty, but cold. Alice shivered. She made sure baby Shirley was tucked up snugly in her beautiful silver cross pram. She was glad her friend's house was just down the road. Even with their coats and head scarves on it was cold enough to give them all red noses.

'Oh it's lovely of you to come and sit with me Alice; I get so lonely now our Cyril's gone. I used to moan about him while he was here,' Mabel said. 'And now he's gone.' Tears glazed her eyes.

Alice comforted her:

'You were the best wife you could have been, and nursed him for years. We all moan about *them,* don't we girls? It's okay as long as they don't hear us.'

The girls laughed. Their dad ruled the house in his strict way in the short time that he was there, between long hours working and long hours pubbing it. But he never really knew much about what went on in the house.

***

About six miles away in Exhall, Les Allen ran anxiously into his house:

'They're coming tonight!' he bellowed. **'They're really coming tonight!!!'**

This stout, strong man looked at his precious family; his wife Maud, two pretty adolescent daughters and three young sons. He scooped up the youngest – three year old Roy, and put him on his shoulders.

'Come on! **COME ON!'**

The sense of urgency in his voice galvanised his family into action. Maud and the elder children grabbed nearby blankets and coats.

'Come on, come on! **Hurry up!'** he

bellowed. Maud opened the back door. They had built an Anderson shelter in the back garden; a small corrugated steel dome over a hole in the ground, covered in soil like a pig sty, often flooded with water. 'No.....over the fields,' Les commanded. 'We'll be safer over the fields. *Come on!'*

As they scurried over the nearby fields they could see black distant specks peppering the sky. They could hear a low droning like a swarm of bees. The specks quickly became a flight of swallows. The family huddled down in the wet, muddy dip of a hedge and pulled the blankets over them. Les still doubted their safety. They lived near an industrial estate and fuel depot.

Suddenly, large bomber planes were right above them! Flying low, the bombers could see them – it would only take one!!!

Silently praying, clinging together, they watched the awesome herd of death machines fly just above their heads. Straight! Determined! On their merciless mission. More and more and more; a seemingly endless aerial stampede – around 500 bombers droned on - all converging on about one square mile – COVENTRY!

***

'Would you pour the tea, Alice? I've got some of my blackberry cordial for the girls. I'll warm it up, they look cold.' Mabel poured some into a saucepan on the range. Alice went to pin back the curtains before settling down. Horrible black blackout curtains behind the flowery chintz ones; were they really necessary?' she wondered.

'The cordial's ready,' Alice said.

'No it's not even bubbling yet,' replied Mabel

'Well what's that strange sound then?'

'What sound?' Mabel was getting a bit deaf.

'That drone, it's getting louder.'

Alice's stomach turned queasy then lurched as the realisation of the sound wacked her. Unnerving sirens screamed their warning.

'Come on! Under the stairs!'

Alice snatched baby Shirley from the pram; her crying wail joined the siren in terrifying harmony as Alice ushered the startled little group into the sloping recess under the stairs.

The low drone became a crescendo, above and all around them.

The frozen children started to cry. Above the crying came a whistling sound then weoooosh! Crash! The house shook! Weeoosh. Crash! Weeoosh. Crash! Weeoosh. Crash! Weeoosh. Crash! A loud piercing whistle …. Deadly, eternal quiet. It was above them. This was the end!

Alice pulled the girls under her on the floor and clutched Mabel's hand. Crash! Alice wee'd herself, then tears and snot dripped down her face as the house shook and rattled but didn't collapse on top of them.

'It's okay,' her voice autopiloted, 'they've missed us. The worst is over.' she stroked the girl's heads reassuringly.

But it was far from over! Wave after wave after wave after wave after wave after wave of savage hate came crashing down whilst the trembling prey lay petrified clinging together on the floor.

Bombing intervals were interspersed with the screaming of sirens, ambulances, fire engines, people.

The mission aptly named '*moonlight* sonata' had one aim – to raze the city of Coventry to the ground!

***

Maud Allen, like many, watched from the field, terrified not just for herself and her children but mostly for her husband. He had gently covered his family with a blanket, all huddled up together like a mother dog and puppies; and set off towards the inferno – to help!

First parachute flares were dropped to highlight the buildings; then booby- trapped incendiary bombs, throwing out white metal shards, knocked out the utilities (gas, electric, water) and created over two hundred fires. About two hours later, 9.30 pm a wave of high explosive bombs stranded Coventry from the outside world as it cut out telephone lines and houses and buildings dropped like cardboard, blocking roads.

With the roads blocked and cratered, water mains burst, gas mains blowing up – the firefighters didn't stand a chance. But they never stopped trying.

Gun defence was low as the city was in a dip and normally blanketed by fog which helped to protect it - but not tonight.

Air mines with tremendous explosions knocked roofs off for incendiary bombs to drop in, causing firestorms and roasting…people!

By 1.30 am the flames were so intense that the molten red that lit up the sky could be seen 100 miles away

But still it went on and on and on and on….

The relatively unscathed bombers completed the most devastating aerial attack in Britain's history. A new word was proudly announced in the German language: 'coventriert,' translated 'coventried,' to describe the new level of destruction.

Finally, at dawn, after this night of hell, the sweet finale 'all clear' siren sang out.

***

The Allen family minus one returned home on heavy legs after their longest night ever. Les, or 'Capel' as he was called, had instructed them to stay put until it was well over, as bombers returning home often dropped any spare bombs they had left. Once inside Maud got the living room fire blazing and they all sat around. It gave them much needed warmth but reminded them of where their dad had gone. They just sat staring at the flames in subdued silence. They sat and sat... all day. Finally about tea time Maud broke the silence:

'I'll warm the rabbit stew up.'

They hadn't eaten for over 24 hours but no-one had an appetite.

The morbid silence was interrupted by the front door slamming.

'Stay here,' Maud commanded. Unusually they did as they were told.

In the hallway her large, strong, brave husband covered in ash and blood stood trembling. She hugged him. Tears came down their cheeks simultaneously. This was a man and a woman who never cried. Capel was able to mutter a few words:

'Heads off…children…'

'Shhh, don't talk.'

She hugged him again:

'Come, I'll run you a bath.'

She helped him undress and get in the bath. Battling all night then day to save people amidst unspeakable heat and terror had reduced him to a dithering wreck.

Having him back had renewed her strength. She gently rubbed him with a towel and dressed him then returned to the children:

'Yer fairther's back, now come on dish up the dinner.'

With hearty smiles they noisily jostled around the table. Sheila fetched the stew pot and Joyce helped dish up while Maud worriedly fetched Capel. She'd never seen anything affect her husband like this. He'd let her bath and dress him like a baby and now was just staring into space:

'Come on,' she commanded: 'Your dinner's on the table.'

She led him to the table and sat him down. Everyone stopped eating, once again immobilised except for their saucer eyes converging on their father.

He was just staring vacantly up into space. Eventually his eyes dropped, taking in the vision of his lovely, lovely family; so vulnerable and needing him; all waiting to see what he would do. He couldn't disappoint: He banged his heavy fist on the table, shaking it and making everyone tense up:

'We'll bloody show em,' he said assertively then banging the table again:

'WE'LL BLOODY SHOW EM!!!'

Three year old Roy stood up on his chair angelically, his blue eyes sparkling through his baby curls:

'We'll buddy sow 'em,' he shouted. He banged his little fist down hard, hitting the side of his plate. Rabbit stew catapulted all over his face. Everyone hooted with hysterical laughter. Things were back to normal.

Or were they……..?

The night of carnage, intended to raze the city of Coventry to the ground and terrify it's people into submission, had stoked - *the fires of revenge!*

Chapter 2.

WHERE'S WALLY?

After 11 long hours of praying through the Coventry night blitz, dawn broke. Mabel's front door had been blown off, shattered glass covered the floor by the window frame, but it didn't matter, *nothing* mattered; they were *alive - they were all alive!*

Alice's relief returned to anxiety as she thought of her husband, Wally. He wasn't perfect but she was so proud to have him as a husband. Was Wally alive?

The thought of losing him was unthinkable. She remembered her own impoverished childhood. Her father had died, leaving her mother with 12 daughters and a son. They would rather have died than go to the much feared workhouse where many children did die. Their mother got a job skivvying in a big house and used to bring bones and scraps home to boil up for their dinner. On Sundays, Alice and some of her sisters would walk 5 miles to a bakery to get sacks of stale bread. A gang of boys would pelt them with stones and call them horrible names because they were so poor. She had large, painful bunions on her feet from wearing painfully fitting shoes. But she had survived.

She just had to know that Wally was safe. Mabel set about organising the children with food and drink and getting them to help clear up the glass and change the baby, whilst Alice set off to search for her husband.

The night had been terrifyingly noisy but Alice was still stunned by the scene that she stepped into. It was unreal- like being in a horror film. Her mind numb with shock. Her weak legs took her from one scene of burning hell to another. This scale of aerial destruction had never been witnessed before. The once proud city was reduced to charred smoking rubble. Firemen and Air Raid Wardens had battled on but with no water supply... buildings were still in flames. Smoking, molten hot metal tram lines were arched up in the air. The pavements were hot, the air thick with choking asphalt and smoke. The service men were exhausted from battling on all night, but they had to keep going. Gas mains had to be turned off, sand thrown at the fires, but most urgently, rubble had to be dug up to see if anyone was alive, wounded seen to. Alice approached her beloved house in a daze. It was no longer there, only a pile of rubble. Her stomach turned over, she wretched. Most of the row of houses were now a pile of charred, smoking rubble. She started to shake. What if she and the children hadn't gone to keep Mabel company? Her neighbours...... Wally! Had he managed to get out of the house before .....! He was going to the corner pub. Blind panic! Somehow her legs took her further down the street towards the pub. A group of soot covered, bloody ARP Wardens were digging up bits of bodies next to the pub, but all that remained of the friendly, sing-along, corner pub was....... a deep bomb crater......this couldn't be happening, not to them... not in England. Alice blacked out.

'Alice....Alice......she was dreaming; Wally was calling her. Wally had never let her be ill; even after childbirth she had got out of bed to make sure he had his dinners and cups of tea. He was so capable and popular in public but with her he was a needy toddler. Her head shook. She opened her eyes to see a sooty face staring into hers – Wally!

He had been digging with the other men but in her blind panic, she hadn't seen him.

'Alice what are you doing, bloody fainting. Come on gal buck up!' She sat up and took a deep breath, still not quite in touch with reality. 'Now, me and the lads need a cup of tea. We haven't stopped all night while you've been in Mabels and now you're just bloody fainting. Can't you see there's an emergency on? Everything's gone Al – the cathedral, the shops, the hospital's been bombed – everything!'

She felt ashamed. She'd never fainted before. She still felt woozy.

'There's no water for tea Wally. I tried at Mabel's.' He looked exasperated:

'Look, woman!' He pointed to a tea wagon that had just arrived. 'Come on Alice, get in the queue, I'm digging for any survivors. Then see to this lot; they're homeless.' A group of people sat on a broken wall, looking like zombies, covered in ash, staring silently into space.

'I'm sorry Wal...I thought you were in the pub,' her voice was tearful.

'Don't be bloody stupid Al you know I'm in the ARP.' He touched his silver Air Warden Patrol badge proudly 'I weren't having me night off with this happening.' At last his ARP training had given him important work. Up until now he'd just been checking that people had put up their blackout curtains properly.

'But Wal didn't you want to know that your own family were alive?'

'Alice, stop being bloody stupid. We need some tea. Martin here's a messenger.'

A young lad about 14 years old smiled at her sheepishly. It was his job to run around whilst bombs were falling and fire storms raging, taking messages back and forth between emergency services. His family must have been sick with worry.

'He looked in your broken window for me and said you were feedin the babby.'

Alice blushed. Martin blushed redder under his sooty face. Alice had been breastfeeding and he'd felt too embarrassed to speak. He'd tried again later, only to see prim and proper Mabel using a biscuit tin as a toilet.

Wally continued: 'Now get in the bloody tea queue, we've got lives to save.' Alice knew there was no chance of a hug or kiss in front of the other men; Wally's self- esteem was more important than anything, but when they were alone he would be loving and needing her again.

In the queue of rubble, she still felt like she was in a film, that it wasn't all real, but her heart was beginning to pump iron back into her limbs. It was strange how Wally's bossiness did that to her and made her feel more able to cope.

'A bit like Churchill,' she thought.

She took the tray of tea back for the diggers. They gulped it down. They had been working frantically all night with the fierce heat of the fires, gas mains exploding and bombs dropping. But now was no time to stop. Who knows how many people were trapped and dying under the smoking debris.

'Take that lot up to Mabel's!' Wally commanded, looking at the zombies. 'I'll make sure you get supplies when they arrive.'

'Would you all like to follow me please,' she said nervously, taking the hand of a small child and the arm of an old man with a walking stick.

If Churchill was in any doubt about how the Coventry people would react to disaster, he would have been reassured by the behavior of this shy woman.

During these war years of long ration queues, people had got into the habit of joining queues to see what was at the other end. By the time Alice got to Mabel's her queue of zombies had multiplied considerably. She stopped outside Mabel's open doorframe and looked at them. There were at least 30 of them now …. and 3 dogs and a budgie in a cage – all silent, suffering from shock. Oh dear, well, Mabel had said she wanted visitors….. Alice pointed to a young boy pushing a pram:

'In you go. Babies and small children in first.'

She looked in the pram to check that the baby was okay as it went past. Two piglets looked up at her. The young boys pleading eyes prevented her from stopping him. 'Oh dear,' she thought,

'What would Mabel think?'

The thought brought on a nervous laugh.

Chapter 3.

LADY LANE.

Like most things, good or bad – the war ended.

Shirley Thompson was now 5 years old. She watched as a conveyor belt of huge tanks victoriously paraded down the main road near her home in Longford. Frightened by these colossal war machines and the noise, she twirled her fingers round her long auburn plaits. Loud noise always frightened her. From infancy she had learned to run and sit under the living room table at the sound of sirens and bangs. Her large, frightened brown eyes anxiously looked for her dad. Spotting him on the other side of the road, in panic, she tried to run to him. In the nick of time a soldier scooped her up, saving her from tragically being flattened by a tank. He handed her back to the care of her family!

Lady Lane was the only home Shirley remembered, but she knew about her former home in George Street, and that *terrible* night; her ears were ever alert; her young brain soaked up adult conversation.

Her mother, Alice, although not normally religious, had quietly but desperately prayed:

'Please God if you keep my family safe I'll never complain again about anything EVER again!'

And she kept her pledge, meekly accepting...everything!

Shirley had seen what might have happened to the family. Her elder sisters took her to visit granny Thompson near the centre of Coventry. They showed her St Marks church where she had had a lovely christening, then further on they all sat outside the 'Rose and Woodbine,' pub and had a ginger nip to drink and a bag of crisps with a little bag of salt in. They saw a massive crater in the ground, made by a German bomb. The hole had once been another pub - the one that *they'd* been invited to the night that it was bombed. Further on there was a lovely boating pool, The Swanswell. This had been a main source of water for the firemen.

Indeed they were extremely lucky to be alive and to find a home quickly. The blitzing of Coventry had left the family with nothing, along with about 3000 homeless people, as over 2000 houses were destroyed and over 40,000 homes suffered some damage. Even some of the air raid shelters deep in the ground had suffered direct hits, killing everyone. Many families moved in with relatives. Hundreds of tents were set up in the grounds of Coombe Abbey – tents to live in at the start of the British winter. The government was worried. Coventry seemed to have had a nervous breakdown. The country watched to see how the people would react. Thousands seemed to be leaving the city, worried that the bombers would return.

The government's worry turned to immense national pride, as, just a day or so after the bombing, thousands of homeless adults made their way, through still smouldering rubble, to go to work in munitions factories with no roofs or windows. They worked through the cold, wet winter in wellies and with umbrellas, they worked harder than ever!

The Thompson family had made their way to Alice's

mothers small cottage, about 3 miles from the city centre, where they felt a bit safer, and, as soon as a house had come up to rent at the other end of that street. They eagerly moved in.

A nice spot, surrounded by fields and just down the road from Alice's mum and sister Florry. But what a terrible lowering of standards the house was. It was the end of a terraced row of similar houses, facing a brick wall. The black front door and windows were slightly rotten and the upstairs bedroom window cracked. The downstairs consisted of just one room. A curtain suspended from the ceiling closed off the only washing facilities – a large, white Belfast sink used for flannel washes and hair washing; that is when it hadn't got smelly chitterlings soaking in there, as it was the only sink in the house. Water was boiled in a copper for baths, and the four girls shared the hot water in front of the fire once a week, while their dad went out; taking it in turns to sit in the small tin bath.

In the rest of the room, the family managed to install an old table and chairs and a blue chequered oilcloth tablecloth. This was for eating dinners on, doing school homework, preparing meals, ironing - everything; the treasured Bakelite radio was also kept there. A ripped, brown leather settee with a spring showing completed the furniture. The fireplace had a little side oven for cooking. The fire always had to be lit however hot the summer, as it was the only means of boiling the kettle or cooking the dinner or warming the iron. This made it impossible to keep milk from going sour. The family mostly drank their tea black. Upstairs were two bedrooms, one for the parents and one for the children. Luckily they only had four girls. Much larger families now survived in these houses. The children's bedroom was really cold as the broken window was never mended. In winter their mother bathed their eyes with tea because the frost stuck their eyelashes together. The toilet was round the back of the house, at the bottom of the back yard, shared by next door's large family. It always stank; in winter it would fill up to the top with frozen poo and Shirley would often run there in the rain to find that someone else was in there. She hated it, especially as she couldn't always get back in her own house quickly because she couldn't yet reach the latch.

True to her promise, Alice accepted her lot meekly and gratefully.

Dissidence amongst her offspring was met with reminders of 'how lucky' they were, and they were told of people in Europe starving.

The lucky one in the family with this arrangement was their father 'Walter' or 'Wally' as he was known. He had a decent job at the Rolls Royce car factory and a family that lived in a slum in poverty and crept around quietly trying to please him. Alice never challenged his behavior. She was not unique in that – to 'obey' their husband was part of the marriage vows of women. Traditionally, keeping a man well fed and healthy was necessary as women and children without a man had often starved or, in the past, gone to the dreaded workhouse. It was just the norm for many families. The household income was mostly spent at the pub where Wally was very generous and popular, as he also was at work where he *never* had a day off ill. He had been idolised at home as a child and now his godlike status continued. He didn't question the fairness of this status quo. Blinkered, leaving the household business to his wife, he probably didn't even know about some of the hardship endured by his family. His meat, potatoes, two veg and gravy dinner was always waiting for him when he got home. The smell of it made the children dizzy with longing. Still, they got the dripping made from the meat fat on their toast or potatoes. They had chicken for Christmas dinner and shared an egg on Sundays; eggs were in shorter supply after the war than during it. Wally always had a good suit and starched white shirt and never knew that the suits travelled frequently to the pawn shop to be retrieved on payday. He wasn't lazy, as well as being a good worker at work, he had an allotment near his house where he grew vegetables for the family and reared the odd pig. With rationing, the family was allowed to keep one pig for their family and this feasting was the highlight of the year. Occasionally they would also have a rabbit. At 5 years old Shirley, (always eager to join in and have a go), could skin a rabbit. She had to cover the eyes as they were too upsetting, but then slit the fur down the middle and took it off - like taking off a babygro. The resulting rabbit stew was pure gourmet luxury for the wife and children who didn't even have meat once a week but watched the master of the house's daily indulgence. It was as if he had put blinkers on so that he could no longer clearly see the family deprivations and he spent very little time there. Maybe this was how he coped with the massive drop in standards from his town house to this drab, dilapidated room full of girls; how he longed for a boy. The family never starved but Shirley, like many children then, was always hungry. Her favorite treat was condensed milk on bread but she also enjoyed pig's trotters and even ate the chitterlings, although the preparation of these was sickening; they were made from pig's intestines. The intestines were fixed to the tap and the poo rinsed out with water, a few times a day for a week, then they were boiled. They stank the place out .....but when you're hungry enough!

Wally wasn't the only one who didn't spend much time in the house, Shirley loved to be outdoors whatever the weather. She didn't like the bad weather to be in her bedroom though. She slept by the cracked window that was tied up with an old belt, but in the wind, rain and snow it often flapped open. It wasn't really, in the order of things, her place to be by the window again but Shirley always looked after little Christine. Then there was Jean 4 years older and the eldest Betty (15), who all slept in the double bed covered with a coarse, grey blanket which was pulled back and forth like a ping –pong ball. Shirley had a real soft spot for little Christine. They were close in age and looked alike with auburn hair, freckles and brown eyes whereas the eldest two had raven black hair and blue eyes. That's where the similarity ended though, Shirley was much tougher than Christine. She always wondered if it was because she had had all Christine's inoculations as well as her own. Because they looked alike, when Christine cried their mother used to ask Shirley to go and have the jabs for her.

Even with four in the bed Shirley's nose used to freeze by the window and wake her. No wonder she always got up early.

She took off her mum's old dress that she wore to bed and pulled her only set of clothes on, then her boots. She wondered why she always seemed to have boots in summer and sandals in winter but her mum said that she was lucky to have footwear that fitted and didn't hurt. Seeing her mum's painful bunions she could see her point. As soon as she reached the fields she would take them off anyway and run barefoot and carefree all day.

Some warm black tea and a piece of bread and dripping, a quick wipe of her teeth with a rag rubbed in chimney soot and spat out in the sink, and she was off to play; free to roam. In stark contrast to her home, her playground was full of wonder and beauty.

Over the fields she picked a large bouquet of wild flowers for her mum. She knew that they wouldn't last long though. The roaring coal fire in the living room withered the flowers within a day. She strolled back towards home with them. Many of the houses that she passed had front gardens with beautiful flowers in. She admired them wistfully. They hadn't got any at home. But, she thought there was a bit of soil by the front of the house where cobble stones were missing; flowers would look lovely there. No-one was about yet. Some of the gardens were brimming with flowers. Using a

41

bit of wood that she found, she dug carefully under the roots. She just took one from each garden; no one would miss them! Excitedly, she held her dress up at the front and filled it with the beautiful flowers, all different colours and shapes of bells and stars. What treasure, what joy! She hurried back as carefully as she could. Her lovely mother deserved flowers.

Alice was horrified. The penalties in her younger days for stealing had been terrible. Even if you were starving, you didn't steal. She took little Shirley back to each house and made her, red- faced, knock on each door and, in a tiny stammering voice, apologise then replant the flowers. Alice was determined: they may be poor, but they were going to uphold high standards!

Shirley went back over the fields alone and sat under a bush feeling very forlorn.

She was not alone for long; a cry like a baby interrupted her thoughts of shame and self-pity. She jumped up and delved around. Under a bush, behind a stump were two tiny, weeny kittens – a black and white and a tabby. They were so tiny and so, so *soft*.

They snuggled up to her and they all comforted one another. Sitting there, feeling needed; feeling their tiny, pounding heartbeats and their warm softness was pure ecstasy. Shirley sat there most of the day, singing them lullabies and telling them stories whilst waiting for their mother to come back. She tried sitting some distance away in case she was putting the mother off. Still no mother cat appeared, and the tiny kittens cried like babies every time she moved away. Daylight began to fade. She shouldn't be out in the fields now, it would soon be dark - but she couldn't *leave them*!

Alice was starting to worry. Shirley had been really embarrassed and upset. It wasn't like her not to come home for food and it was getting dark. She was never disobedient about being back before dark. The hours went by. Finally, there was a weak tap on the door. Relieved, the anguished mother opened it to see Shirley with the two tiny kittens a few paces behind her.

'They followed me mam, from up the fields.'

Well the tiny kittens could barely walk and the

fields were quite a distance, so Alice knew that Shirley hadn't yet quite learnt how to be honest. It was a daily struggle to feed the children never-lone animals. Alice's heart melted. Little Shirley hadn't got anything nice.

'Well you don't have to feed cats. They can look after themselves. They could live in the outbuildings round the back. ...And you can give them a drop of milk every day,' she added kindly. Her child's face glowed with indescribable joy.

Chapter 4.

THERE'S NO PLACE LIKE HOME!

Icy raindrops showering her freckled nose woke Shirley up abruptly. She sighed heavily. She'd been in deep slumber cuddled up to her younger sister Christine. The two elder sister, Betty and Jean who also shared the king size bed were still sleeping soundly; their raven –black hair plaited and pinned to the top of their heads with hairgrips. From their nose down they were covered by a coarse, grey blanket and old coats. Most nights there was a bit of a breeze from the broken window, and a few drops of rain often hit Shirley's face when it rained heavily – her father said that it was healthy - but it was worse than usual. The relentless wind had clattered the window pane all night, finally snapping the ripped pair of nylon stockings that had been tied to the headboard of the bed and fastened to the broken window latch. It had happened before, so Shirley knew what to do and now that her pillow was wet she thought she might as well

45

get up. At least her eyes weren't stuck together today.

She shivered and put one of the old coats on , over the old flowery dress of her mums that she wore to bed, then knotted the stockings and re-fastened the window as well as she could. She shivered again; she needed a wee. She stooped on the bucket in the corner and tried to wee as quietly as she could, which isn't easy on a tin bucket, then she crept through her parent's room, past her snoring father, and down the creaky stairs. It's strange how everything seems a lot louder when you're trying hard to be quiet. She felt a sense of triumph at the bottom of the stairs at managing not to wake anyone. A big smile crossed her face; her mother was already up and had got the coal fire going – much needed warmth, and her mother un- shared!

Alice was dressed already in her long flowery pinny and soft wide slippers, with little cuts in for the large, painful bunions on her feet; her hair was neatly rolled up in curlers with a hairnet over. She'd emptied the heavy ash tray from under the fire down the back garden and filled up the coal scuttle by the fireplace. Shirley watched, impressed, as her mother livened up the fire by putting a page of newspaper over the opening; the fire made a low roaring noise as it tried to suck in the newspaper. Alice had developed the knack of pulling the scorched newspaper off just at the right moment, (another few seconds and the paper would have caught fire), revealing lively, dancing, warming flames. Shirley rubbed her hands gleefully in front of the fire then the two continued their morning ritual: Alice boiled the large black kettle on the fire and made the tea, black, because yesterday's milk was full of lumpy bits and the milkman hadn't yet arrived. She wished he didn't bother coming – his horse always did its smelly business in front of her house. It was useful for their allotment, but she didn't always want to run and shovel it up and carry it down the bottom of the garden.

'I'll make the toast, mam.' It was Shirley's favourite job. She got the heavy metal poker and moved some of the coal at the front of the fire to reveal glowing embers; high flames would burn the toast. Then she picked up the brass toasting fork, which was about as long as her arm, and carefully pushed the four prongs through a slice of bread and balanced the bread just above the red glowing embers and toasted it one side, then the other, being careful to push the prongs through the same holes when she turned it, otherwise the bread would collapse in the middle creating a large hole that wouldn't stay on the fork. The bread didn't toast evenly; the bit round the holes always went black as did other bits that random flames caught, but this gave it a tasty, smoky flavour – some butter or for a treat today, pig dripping, and Shirley was well happy.

Not much time to savour though; her mother needed an errand today before school:

'Be a love and fetch me some snuff will you our Shirl, I've run out. And can you get a quarter for granny Randle as well?'

Not really a question. Shirley sighed quietly – it was a horrible wet day. Well she'd better hurry, she didn't want to be late for school. She got a rag and stuck it up the chimney to get some soot, then rubbed her teeth to clean them, swilling her mouth with a mug of water and spitting it into a bowl – the large Belfast sink had smelly chitterlings soaking in it. She got dressed in her one faded set of clothes, with a pin to hold her knickers up; she wished her mum would get round to putting new elastic in them; well at least she'd got some her friend next door often hadn't. She re-plaited her long auburn hair; her mum would have done this but Shirley had a real independent streak and had quite enough of her mum messing with her hair. Every evening Alice sat the girls by the front window to catch the light and scraped their head with a nit comb while they protested and groaned. They felt really embarrassed if anyone saw them but the embarrassment at school would have been worse if they'd got nits. They'd also have to have their lovely hair cut off, so they knew it was necessary pain. Finally little Shirley got her eldest sister Betty's silk scarf and gave her hair a rub, just like her sister – to make it shine.

Her mother gave her the snuff money and the bus fare:

'Get me two quarters of SP no 1, please.' She didn't really need to say anything, Shirley had been regularly going on this errand since she turned six years old but looked reluctant today.

'You can have a penny for going,' her mum bribed.

Shirley's eyes gleamed:

'Thanks mam I'll get a pennyworth of spec.' For a penny you could get three or four pieces of fruit that were bruised, over-ripe or speckled. Alice smiled, little Shirl would do anything for food.

'They'll be calling you Gobble- Girty again,' she teased.

Shirley put her hat, coat and boots on and set off into the dark drizzly day. The shop was about four miles away on the bus, which she caught on the main Coventry road just round the corner. It wasn't yet open when she got there, but Shirley knew what to do. She went up the side of the shop and knocked on the door, of the house at the back; She had to bang loudly because the lady who answered was a bit deaf, luckily she always served her, maybe for the sale, but more likely out of kindness for the skinny, wet little girl who had come so far on her errand.

On the bus back Shirley couldn't help trying the snuff. It was brown powder, like gravy browning; she took a pinch, shut her mouth and breathed it up her nose, a quick deep snort, like she'd seen her mother do; it sent a strange rush to her head and made her sneeze. Her mother knew that she did it because it was difficult to get the brown stain off your nostrils, but as always Alice never protested.

Errand delivered, Shirley ran off to school just in time to see Miss Brown in the playground ringing the large, brass hand bell, summoning the children to queue up at the school door.

Shirley gave Miss Brown a big smile as she passed through the door into the school attached to Longford church. She dearly loved this little school. Everyone hung their coats up, then went into the large room for assembly and prayers with the Headmaster; then, two sliding doors were pulled across to divide the room into three classrooms. High Victorian windows prevented distractions and sunshine from outside, like a prison. A small iron burner which the teacher stoked up threw a bit of heat out; for some reason the children's milk was put by it making it warm and curdly. Well-used wooden desks with ink wells, a blackboard, high bare walls, children in tatty, faded clothes. Why did Shirley love it so much? It certainly wasn't the dinners; even though she was always hungry and rarely got meat, Shirley wouldn't have the free dinners. She had tried but was embarrassed by the knives and forks – she'd only ever used a spoon at home. Then there was the terrible overpowering smell of the over-steamed cabbage, more pungent than men's sweaty socks. She preferred to run home and have a jacket potato, which was a bit hit and miss – hot and soft if the fire was going well - a bit hard if not, but nevertheless enjoyed with her mum.

The drabness and austerity of the school classroom in no way dried up the enthusiasm and love of learning which gushed out of the teachers and was soaked up by its star pupil, ever eager to please and hungry for attention. In assembly and music, Shirley sang as loud as she could, even though, tone deaf, she never quite mastered the tunes. At reading she was much more successful. She shared her precious skills and taught a little group of gypsy children to read in class; they loved her helpful, kind manner and the teachers clearly adored her. Shirley got all the lead parts in the plays, not merely through favouritism, more because she was the only one who learnt all her words, and everyone else's. When she was still only seven the school had a problem, she had read every book they had. The teachers kept giving her a penny of their own money for bus fare and sending her to fetch more books from the library; an errand she was well used to, as she fetched Sexton Blake and Charles Dickens books for her mother's afternoon read. For winning exams, the teachers would give her 3d (again out of their own pockets) and unreserved praise. Two prizes and she had enough money to go to the pictures. One of the teachers, who had no children of her own sometimes took Shirley home for tea and to meet her sister, the other Miss Brown.

Certain special religious festivals were spent happily country dancing in the grounds of the adjoining vicarage. However, one school trip was less successful: The whole school of 40 – 50 pupils was instructed to bring a pair of pants, navy if they'd got them, and a vest if they wanted to. This was their Physical Education kit in which they regularly shivered in the playground. Unlike P.E. they also had to bring a spare pair of pants. A problem for some who had to borrow from siblings who then had none to wear. The trip was to Livingstone Road Baths - to learn to swim!

With noisy excitement, the children got ready in the Bath's changing rooms, then walked through nervously. A small blue pool of water greeted them; the first three children jumped in excitedly:

'Ooh it's lovely,' they whooped. The teacher pushed her way through the crowd. She laughed:

'That's to wash your feet in. You won't all fit in there. Come on. Follow me everyone!'

Apart from the local stream, the most water that any of

them had ever seen was a tin bath. Seeing the vast blue of the baths the whole school froze, terrified, pressing their backs to the wall. The well-intentioned, flustered teachers didn't manage to get anyone in until the third visit.

Shirley eventually mastered the basic mechanics of swimming, but in a very tense robotic form. She always found it a bit traumatic and kept her head well above water, but she discovered a new delight at the baths. Her father and elder sisters often went there and now, whenever she had enough money, she could treat herself, but not to swim – she went for a bath. As young as she was and as difficult as it was, she was very clean. At home she had kettles of hot water and flannel washes in the kitchen sink behind the curtain or with a bowl if the sink was full. If there was no kettle of hot water because the fire had gone out, she would use cold water - even to wash her hair. Once a week, on Sunday a copper was boiled and their dad went out while the four girls took it in turns to get in the tin bath by the fire, sharing the bath water.

She started to go to Livingstone Road slipper baths

with her cousin Barbara, a bit older than herself but waif –like and younger looking. For a penny they would be given a small bar of white soap and a white towel each. The baths were in little cubicles 1/3 full of very hot water. The girls didn't realise that *they* were supposed to put the cold water in, so sat happily singing on the benches until the water was cool enough to get in.

Barbara lived at the opposite end of Lady Lane. Her parent's had died and the brothers and sisters had all been adopted by other members of the family; Barbara by childless aunt Florry who still lived with Shirley's granny Randle. She was now one of Shirley's favourite out- of -school playmates. Shirley's sister Christine was two year's younger and had been frightened off a bit by their experiences. One in particular; sitting by the river two shire horses had appeared from nowhere and jumped right over the girl's heads and into the water. Christine felt safer with her mum. But Shirley just couldn't bear to stay in the house whatever the risks. She had worried that she might also lose Barbara as a roaming friend after one early morning escapade: The two little girls had just been through the fields to the rag and bone abattoir to get some maggots for fishing. The maggots crawled under the door and they soon filled a jar. They were walking back chatting happily, arm in arm, when suddenly a fierce looking man with a long beard and long wild hair jumped from behind a bush - *naked*! He chased them, shouting madly! They ran all the way home, terrified and, shaking, they gabbled their tale to Alice. She didn't even stop ironing:

'Oh don't worry about him, he's harmless enough. Poor man's been like that since the war. They say he's suffering from shell shock. He probably thought you were attacking him in his sleep. He's from a good family but chooses to roam the fields. Every now and then the authority's take him away and he comes out all clean in a nice suit, but then goes back to his strange ways.'

The girls saw him quite regularly after that, as he would turn up at the downstairs window of their homes and shove his tin mug in grunting. Some bread and a mug of tea, handed through the window and he would leave grunting more happily. Many men became tramps after the war, particularly if they had lost homes and families – this one had become permanently scarred.

The experience didn't deter plucky little Barbara, neither did her annoying cough. The two girls continued with their very early morning walks because they were desperately hoping that the fresh air and exercise would rid little Barbara of her cough. But, it didn't, the cough just got worse and worse and her eyes became sunken and dark. Thin little Barbara was diagnosed with TB, a common, very infectious and often fatal disease. She was sent away to a sanatorium.

At school, they said a prayer for her! Shirley missed her so much. The sanatorium was in Leamington; poor little Barbara was seriously ill and a long way from her friends and family. She would have few visitors at this painful, frightening time. Shirley perked up when her teacher, kind as ever, asked her if she would like to go and visit Barbara in a car. Not many people had one. However, because it was such an infectious disease; Shirley wondered if her parents would let her go. She asked her mother and received the usual anxious reply:

'....just make sure you don't tell your father!'

The clinical, bare walled, sanatorium ward made Shirley shiver. Her pathway was down the centre of two long, long rows of beds. It was all a bit scary. It wasn't just ascetically cold with stark walls and high ceilings, all the windows were wide open for fresh air to lessen the germs; still she'd have to be brave for her cousin. Barbara's bed was right near the far end.

It was well worth going to see little Barbara's face and such a comfort to Shirley to find that Barbara looked Rosier and fatter and was pleased with her surroundings:

'Look at my bed and my lovely white blankets, Shirl,' she was really pleased to show them off.

The kind teacher gave little Barbara presents from the school staff and the class and the two girls giggled and chatted as they had always done, delighted to see one another again. They still really shouldn't have, but hugged each other tightly at the end of visiting time.

Barbara would have to make that hug last. T.B. had a lengthy recovery if at all. But now Shirley just knew that she would recover... eventually! Barbara was a survivor and Shirley could see small specks of that magical fighting spirit back in her eyes.

Back home, and still missing her friend, Shirley spent more time than usual with the local coal merchant's family. They invited her to watch their television. They were the only people Shirley knew who had got one. They took her on lovely outings with them in their car; the only people in the street to have one. She enjoyed helping them with their handicapped daughter. She even loved their toilet. It was just for their family and visitors and so clean. They used newspaper to wipe and Mrs Baxter cut it into neat little squares and hung it on a hook. Shirley loved being with them.

Somehow, Shirley didn't catch T.B. no doubt her 'gobble girty' appetite, her dad's allotment vegetables and massive doses of fresh air helped - but other killers were lurking. The red hot summer of 1947 brought an epidemic of scarlet fever, a real killer. You could catch it by touching the skin of an infected person or an object that they had touched. There was no doubt that Shirley had succumbed. A sore, sandpaper throat, much vomiting, a very red rash and delirious fierce hot fever. It was a real killer and so bad was the epidemic that there was no room in the hospitals. Shirley lay on the ripped living room settee. Sheets soaked in Jeyes fluid were hung around her. Everything was fumigated, even her library book. All the other children in the house were sent to relatives but little Christine wouldn't stop crying to come home and, as ever, Alice gave in.

Shirley fought for her life, in the furnace that her body had become. A doctor came in every day; the financial cost mounted up – doctors weren't cheap. He wasn't pleased:

'Is this all you've got for this poor child to sleep on?' he asked angrily. He shook his head worriedly.

'There'll be no charge!'

At the little church school they said a daily prayer for little Shirley. Most of the street did. Everyone missed this helpful, enthusiastic little girl – the thought of her dying....

Finally....the fever passed!

People came with presents. The Marlowes, her headmaster and his wife, her teachers, her posh aunt who gave her drinks in a china cup and saucer and let her tinkle on the piano. They all bore gifts then had private conversations with her mother, outside. Her mother didn't look happy. What was it? She was getting better and all these lovely gifts. What was wrong with her mother? Shirley was puzzled. Alice had to explain, she spoke quietly:

'...They all want to adopt you Shirl – all of them. They can all give you much more than I can, things you deserve. They all want you. It's up to you to choose which of them you want to live with!'

Shirley's face contorted. She was shocked and deeply hurt.

'Don't you want me mam?' she asked in a tearful voice.

Tears streamed down her face….but not for long. Her strength welled up and she announced her decision:

'THIS... is MY HOME!!!'

Chapter 5.

A BRIDGE TOO FAR!

Shirley slid out of bed, woken by someone rolling over and pushing her half off the bed. In good spirits, because she liked to be first up anyway, she peered out of the cracked window. It looked like it was going to be a nice day. She loved Sundays; she always went to the little chapel over the fields and loved singing and Sunday school, then she'd stop off at the brook and splosh around and catch sticklebacks. Remembering the week before, her enthusiasm died. She slumped down on the bed; she couldn't go to chapel. It was going to be a special remembrance day this Sunday - she just couldn't go. She picked her clothes up off the floor. Tonight her only set of clothes would be washed and hung by the fire to be clean for school the next morning. Today they looked their worse. Faded and a week of wear, they weren't even completely clean. Last week she'd been praised up for coming top in the Sunday school quiz at chapel and had sang her loudest.

Then, walking out of chapel with the other girls, she encountered their un-christian jealousy:

'You got a new dress for next week? WE HAVE! ...   S u r e l y you're not coming like that!' A chorus of titters and sniggers turned Shirley's face as red as her hair.

Pulling her clothes on with heavy arms, she slouched downstairs. As always her mother was there. Alice Thompson always got up with the dawn, a habit formed from having little artificial light. It was the best time of the day. She got a warm fire going for her husband's morning cuppa and tended it all day; even on hot summers days the fire had to be nurtured for cooking and pots of tea. Taking out the ashes on a heavy iron shovel, she was cheered by the magnificent birdsong that only the earliest risers are fortunate to experience. She also got the outside toilet to herself without queuing. But today she was worried that her daughter wasn't her usual self. She usually boinged around like she was full of springs. Even her long auburn hair seemed to bounce as she walked:

'What's up?' she asked.

'I can't go to chapel today,' Shirley's subdued voice answered.

Alice nodded understandingly; she didn't need to ask why-she'd heard some of the other mums bragging about the dresses they were getting their daughters when she joined an unusually long ration queue.

'Well I don't know why you bother with all that religious nonsense anyway. It looks like it's going to be a lovely day and aunt Florry says you can start using her toilet so you don't have to use our dirty hole again.'

'But it's right up the road!' She wasn't easy to cheer up today. This was really out of character. Alice persevered:

'I've got you a really special treat for later. It's come all the way over the sea from Africa.'

Shirley looked at the long yellow crescent shaped object. She'd never seen anything like it.

'It's called a banana! We've got some lovely dripping for on our toast as well. Make us a piece of toast and pour us a cup of tea. There's a love.'

Comforted by the special breakfast and her mother's kind voice, Shirley's self-pity was replaced by curiosity at the pile of bananas in a bowl on the table by her fish. Her spirits rose a little, then dipped. Oh no, her fish had died again! The sticklebacks and minnows that she kept in a large glass pickle jar never lasted long. Possibly because she wasn't told that they needed food. Well, never mind, she could go and get some more today. Her eyes sparkled at the thought of sploshing about in her special brook.

The special mother/daughter time was soon interrupted by Shirley's three sisters then her father. They always seemed to get up all together. Her mother now focused her undivided attention on keeping her father happy. Waiting on his every whim and keeping the rest of the family quiet so that he could eat his breakfast in peace, read the Sunday newspaper and listen to the radio undisturbed before he dressed in his Sunday suit and starched white shirt and went down the pub to spend most of his wages. Even turning the pages of a book had to be done as quietly as possible. It was time for Shirley to get out! Taking her empty jam jar and her prized banana, she gave her mum an ear to ear smile and, on tip-toes, opened the black front door latch and escaped into the bright Sunday morning.

Stepping onto the cobbled street of terraced cottages that made up Lady Lane, she eagerly looked at her banana. It didn't look like anything she'd ever eaten before. Fanny, the next door neighbour was already sitting on her orange box out the front of the house, a fat slouchy woman with enormous cow like breasts that she regularly got out to feed her yearly offspring.

Some of the toddlers were playing with the pebbles in the street dressed only in t-shirts or vests. Shirley looked for Lizzie a bit younger than herself; Lizzie had been born in Coventry hospital in the blitz the night the hospital had been bombed. They were good friends. Lizzie always made Shirley feel fortunate because, as well as her traumatic start in life, Lizzie rarely had underwear. Although Shirley's pants were kept up with a pin because the elastic had snapped, at least she had some, and could enjoy doing hand stands up the wall; And Shirley never got nits. Her mum sat all the girls, embarrassingly in the front window for the light, *every* night and scraped their head with a nit comb before plaiting it tightly. It was a daily ritual that she hated, but she'd have hated it more if she'd got called out at school for the dreaded brown envelope from Nitty Nora, the nickname for the school nurse who checked the pupil's heads regularly. Lizzie never got xmas presents either; Shirley's granny Thompson bought them Charles Dickens books, dolls, fruit and sweets at xmas. The dolls very upsettingly used to break when dropped because they had clay heads, resulting in a lot of tears, but the family enjoyed reading. Granny Thompson had encouraged Shirley to read from a very young age. She had caught the bus to their house once a fortnight, bringing sweets and comics; 'Film Fun,' 'The Beano' and 'The Dandy.' Lizzie often used to get Shirley to read things to her. Shirley smiled at everyone but decided against eating her special banana with them all watching because they probably hadn't got one.

Further up the street, she popped into aunt Florry's. Aunt Florry lived with granny Randle and they had a lot of cats. They didn't have to share their toilet with neighbours and Shirley not only had the privilege of using their clean loo, they gave her a biscuit and a new jam jar for her fishing; she felt well blessed.

Down a dark, dirt path, alongside a churchyard… her portal to another world, and into the lush green fields, full of buttercups smiling up at her. It was great to be alive on such a glorious day. She sang her favourite church song 'All things bright and beautiful,' as she skipped along. Crossing the little wooden bridge over the brook, she decided to go to the top of the hill and eat her banana. Full of happy energy, she clambered up the hill. She was on top of her world…until fat Stewart, as he was cruelly called, came walking along. Although, she had wanted to be alone, she smiled and took a bite out of her banana. It was really bitter and hard, with a softer inside. She choked and spat it out. Stewart had also gone up there to be alone. Taunted a lot about his weight, he now turned predator on the skinny girl, a few years younger than him.

'Ginger nut, ginger tom cat. Don't you even know how to peel a banana?' He stuck his tongue out. Well, that was it! Yes she had got red hair and on occasion the viciousness of a cat. The volcano erupted. She lashed out, just catching him off balance and he rolled down the hill – right down into the squishy mud at the bottom. Pasted with mud and holding his now sprained wrist he ran over the bridge towards home.

Surprised and overwhelmed by her victory, but now feeling shaken, Shirley clambered down to the brook. She spent a lot of time in this little brook. On first contact, the hard pebbles and shockingly cold water stiffened her body up. Then, as her flesh acclimatised she began to enjoy sloshing around in the swirling water; her toes sinking into the bed of soft mud further in; everything else forgotten.

She had become very adept at catching the small fish with her hands, keeping some for her jam jar of river water. Taking care not to cloud the clear water with mud, she spotted a shoal of little black sticklebacks, also enjoying the day. She deftly scooped one up and climbed up the bank to her jam jar. She thought she'd take quite a few in the hope that they'd last longer. Everyone had to sit quietly at home when father listened to the radio; watching her fish was much more interesting than listening to boxing. It was a little part of her brook, with her at home. She clambered up and down the bank, until she felt like a rest then sat on the river bank, her legs dangling in the river, the sun warming her body. Willow trees draped both sides of the river, silver birch trees shimmered. Carefree, Shirley undid her long plaits, loosened her hair and leaned back. The warm breeze weaved through her hair. She shook her head defiantly, like a horse that wants to show that it is not totally tame. She succumbed to the symphonic sounds of nature. Minutes, hours, who knows?

Her bliss was interrupted by the sound of voices. Oh no. It was *them*! - the gang of girls in their new frocks on their way to chapel; and they'd all sneer at her again. Fight or flight? Really no question when you have red hair and have just beat someone a lot bigger than you! She was in no mood for their jeering. She stomped over to the highest point of the wooden hump back bridge. Gripping the wooden hand rails either side of her for strength and standing as tall as she could, her corrugated red hair blowing wildly, a smear of mud on her face, she faced the enemy:

'You needn't think you're coming over this bridge. This is my dad's bridge and *you're* not allowed!'

The group had met fat Stewart on the way and heard his story. Mouths open, they retreated without a fight. From the bridge she watched as they took their new shoes and frilly socks off a bit further down the river. Alas, they didn't know the brook like she did and chose a stretch of water where the current knocked you over. She could hear them squealing as they put their feet in the icy water, groaning on the stones and falling over as they got to the middle where the current was strongest; then clambering up the muddy, brambly, bank.

She smiled her victory smile. A cheeky boy's face appeared from behind a bush, laughing. Resting from rabbiting with his dog, he had watched everything.

Wow he'd never seen a girl like this:

'I didn't know the Vikings had landed,' he shouted cheekily.

Something about his cheerful grin and twinkly blue eyes made her smile and blush........ as red as her hair!

Chapter 6.

A MALE WAS BORN – FROG'S HALL, CROW'S NEST.

The boy with the mischievous grin, a wavy mop of blonde hair and bright blue eyes was 'Roy Allen' - although he hadn't got a birth certificate to prove it! His birth certificate merely said:

'A male was born, Frog's Hall, Crows Nest, Warwickshire.' and he thought the place of birth made him sound like a frog. The year: '1937.' He was the fifth child of Maud and Leslie Allen, with two elder brothers and two elder sisters: Starting with the eldest Joyce, Sheila, Leslie, and Don. His parents, like many in those times couldn't afford the three shillings and sixpence for a full birth certificate. The small nameless one, which by law you had to get within a few weeks of the birth, was only threepence or '3d.' then the parents were supposed to return within the year with this temporary piece of paper bearing the registration

number and pay two shillings for the full one. It worked out cheaper to do it this way. Originally the names had been put on the small certificate but people weren't bothering to get the full certificate so names were omitted. Some, like Roy, now ten years old, ended up with just the nameless one.

The place, 'Frog's Hall, Crow's Nest,' sounded like a grand hall in 'Wind in the Willows,' but it was, in fact, an isolated cottage, surrounded by fields with a well and a pond from which the family fetched their water; a chocolate box picture cottage, with foxgloves and dog roses, a vegetable and herb patch. Very beautiful, and loved by the family, but life wasn't easy being miles away from everyone – especially in winter. Water had to be fetched from the well, which sometimes froze over, or the pond. The toilet was outside in a little unheated shed, a barrel with a hole in the bottom and a deep hole in the ground with a plank with a hole cut in it to sit on.

 Shopping had to be fetched from miles away, often in a pram, and giving birth there......!

Not surprisingly the family were overjoyed when they were offered a council house a few miles away. They opened the little wooden gate of 200 Blackhorse Road, Exhall, Bedworth, and entered a neat little front garden with a privet hedge and – a grocery shop....just over the road!!! Slightly cut off from Bedworth and Longford, Coventry, by a long lane one side and a canal bridge and lane the other, Blackhorse road and a few more streets was a community on its own. What a fantastic location – Maud was already in love with it. Her husband's favourite pub, 'The Boat Inn,' (commonly called 'The Old Boat,' or 'The Boat,') was just down the street, a bonus for him. The location would have been enough for them to love the house. They opened the front door excitedly into a large through hall with a little room under the stairs with *a bath and running water*! As she went from room to room Maud was speechless, her senses so overwhelmed – she just couldn't believe that all this luxury was to be theirs; the local council had done them proud. There was a large living room with a fireplace and large storage cupboards and drawers to the side of the fireplace; a good sized kitchen with a proper modern gas stove and a large Belfast sink with two taps one for drinking and one for nice soft rainwater which came from an outside tank, lovely for washing clothes and hair; a separate front room; a back garden with a proper metal coalhouse, large enough to keep a month's coal dry, and a further side garden; *four* bedrooms and last but possibly one of the best features - a toilet, not inside the house but joined on; it had a long chain that you pulled and flushed water. Maud managed to speak at last:

'We could put the paraffin lamp in here, so that it doesn't freeze and I'll crochet a cover to put on the toilet seat,' she beamed.

Her husband agreed, it would be a great place to read his newspapers. The children were delighted. They ran around, flushing the toilet, playing with the taps, switching the electric lights on and off and sliding down the stairs bannister, it was all amazing ; then outside to swing on the gate and meet all the street kids that had come to watch; privacy would be a thing of the past, they were joining the Blackhorse Road community.

At night- time Maud got the happy children bathed; so easy now that she could just turn the bath taps on. They sat rubbing their hair with towels around the warm coal fire, all smelling of green soap; all dressed in long, warm flannelette nighties that she had made. She filled stone hot water bottles with near-boiling water and put them in the beds.

She was delighted with all her new, mod cons, but in the evenings, she chose not to use the electric lights: The flames of the coal fire cast dancing shadows around the room; the children sat watching the changing colours and shapes of the flames, their imaginations whirring whilst dipping their toast in warm milk. Maud didn't even flick the hall light on as she escorted them to bed; candle light was more natural, more relaxing, sleep inducing. The little troupe left the warmth of the living room fire and took two candles in brass candleholders with handles; one for the girl's room and one for the boy's. A ceramic chamber- pot was left in each room under the bed, so that they didn't have to venture downstairs to the toilet.

The children kissed their mother goodnight, said their prayers, then lay on the feather down mattress and pillows, covered with a home- made eiderdown quilt, crammed full of feathers. They watched the relaxing shadows of the candle flickering on the bedroom wall, softly lighting up the gentle smile of Jesus, watching over them from the bedroom pictures. There was another small room – the box room, but this was to be used for storage; no child was to sleep alone; baby Roy, although still officially nameless, would still sleep happy, swaddled and cuddled in his parent's room.

Chapter 7

DROWNING IN FEAR!

Very few cars frequented the street outside 200 Blackhorse road in 1940. Daily deliveries were mostly by horse and cart, with people running out with shovels to collect the steaming, pungent horse manure for their vegetable gardens and allotments. Nevertheless the street was a hive of activity from morning until dark; women chatted over garden hedges, or outside the grocery shop. The street was a safe playground for young children – the elder ones roamed further afield. Young girls pushed real babies in prams and pushchairs; boys played football with anything they could find or marbles.

Now 3 years old, young Roy ran out straight after breakfast, with instructions by his mother to:

'Stay out the front, no wandering off!'

His elder brothers were already out, not wanting to

miss a minute of their day off school. Two jumpers for goalposts each end and a tin can and they were engrossed in a game of six- a- side football in the middle of the road. The numbers were anybody who was there considered good enough to play. Roy climbed upon his wooden front gate and swung backwards and forwards, watching the match, still eating a piece of toast;

'GOAL,' he cheered – he was their best supporter but didn't get chance to be in the team much, unless they were extremely short of players as, in the fierce competition he might get knocked over.

Three boys that Roy hadn't seen before came walking down the street from the other side of the bridge:

'Can *we* play footie, please?' the eldest one shouted.

'No chance, we've got enough and we've already started; we don't want you lot round here so clear off,' someone replied.

It was the answer they thought they might get as they

didn't live in this street and were considered a bit posh, but they still felt dejected as they set off back the way they had come.

Roy watched with interest, if they weren't playing footie perhaps they might play with him. He dropped off the gate and followed them.

They walked down the end of the street and went under the dark canal bridge. They began throwing pebbles in the water, listening to the lovely plopping sound, then hearing their voices reverberate round the cavern-like surround; they started shouting:

'Hello there. Is anybody there? Poo in your pants! Tits and bums!' laughing at the strange, booming sound of their own rude voices.

Roy thought this looked great fun and completely forgot that this area was out of bounds:

'Poo in your pants!' he shouted, giggling.

'Clear off, we don't want any of you lot with us!' They were still angry at their rejection.

'Yes, you get back to your own lot,' a younger one joined in and gave Roy a bit of a push.

Losing his footing Roy fell, whoosh into the icy-cold, grey canal water.

'Quick scarper, they'll kill us!' shouted the eldest, fearfully.

The frightened rabbits ran, not daring to look back; leaving the chubby, baby-faced child floundering in the murky water. Roy was gripped with icy terror, struggling desperately, fighting with all his young strength to stay afloat; trying to shout but just gulping down water, choking, more and more suffocating water, filling his mouth, his nose, his lungs... Finally, all his oxygen and fight depleted, he slumped, lifeless, and grey into the watery graveyard!

Isolated under the dark, canal bridge, nobody had heard him and now he could hear or see nothing; his loved ones oblivious to his fate.

Just a few minutes ago, he had been having such fun!

A man, returning from the pub merrily, though fully

grown, still enjoyed boyhood fun under the canal bridge. He whistled loudly and threw a pebble in the water....plop! His face froze, horrified as he saw a lifeless head bob up!

In he plunged, dragging the heavy, sodden small body to the bank. He pushed it up onto the towpath and struggled up. There didn't seem much point but he had to try; he clasped his arms round the waist from the back and pumped the body, then lay it on his back, head tilted, nose pinched, he breathed into the mouth. He prayed he was doing it right. He'd never had chance to practise his first aid and he'd had a few drinks. Finally, after what seemed like ages, Roy coughed and spluttered and the bluish tint drained from his face. Fate had not yet abandoned the small child. The colour of intense relief poured into his saviours face. Dripping wet, he carried the small, exhausted wet body the short distance up the street full of people to the safety of home - so near and yet so far.

***

Not surprisingly Roy learnt a real fear of water, not

just by day; at night when the sirens screamed the family left the warmth of the house to huddle in the Andersen shelter at the bottom of their garden. The small dome-shaped, metal hidey-hole was built on clay and in the autumn and winter regularly filled up with rainwater as high as his dad's knees. Bailing out water on cold nights, frightened of a bomb landing on their house, or worse - *them*, was abject misery for adults and pure trauma for a small child.

Despite the privations, the children really enjoyed many aspects of their life. As they grew older, they started to roam further afield, but it seemed that Roy was destined to remain at the garden gate. Only his love of animals coaxed him to venture further afield. He couldn't resist taking the dog a walk with the family, and felt safe in the presence of the Alsatian guard dog, even in the Andersen shelter he snuggled up, feeling the warm racing heartbeat of his furry friend. Comforting the dog helped allay his own fears a little.

Summer arrived, and the perils of the nights were forgotten as, by day, the children frolicked; like performing otters in the canals and rivers – except for Roy. His family tried unsuccessfully to persuade him:

'No, I'll get drowned!' He answered.

'We won't let you drown Roy, we'll teach you to swim - look even the dog can swim.'

Don threw a stick in and the dog retrieved it and swam back doggy paddling.

He picked his younger brother up:

'Doggy paddle Roy, that's it you can do it, kick your legs as well.'

Roy had watched everyone swimming and thought he knew what to do but the thought of doing it in the water gripped him with fear.

Don persevered: 'I'll hold you in the water while you practise, I won't let go, I promise.'

Roy trusted Don and gradually, over a few weeks, first dangling his legs in the canal water and kicking, then letting his brother hold him, he progressed to doing his doggy paddle with his brother holding his torso up.

'You can do it Roy, Don encouraged 'but I've promised not to let go so I won't till you say.'

Roy still felt terrified and the fear of trying alone turned his body to heavy stone. The family despaired of him ever getting his confidence back. He was perfectly able, except for the fear.

At home his family talked a lot about courage, facing up to fear, carrying on even when you are frightened. He loved the tale of the spitfires in the recent battle of Britain. The pilots outnumbered, facing the large German planes. They must have been frightened but carried on so courageously to victory.

It had been fear that prompted the boys to run away and leave Roy in the canal drowning. Fear was a major weapon of Hitler, nurtured it grew and grew. Churchill's defiance was a great medicine for alleviating the symptoms of fear. Young Roy knew that he had to find his courage somehow; cowardice was the worst of sins.

One pleasant summer afternoon, he went for a walk with his mother and the dog past the Greyhound Inn; a

88

welcoming pub on the canal towpath at Sutton Stop. They waved to Rose and Joe Skinner, bringing their mule- drawn narrowboat, 'The Friendship,' back to moor near the pub. Joe was more than ready for a pint of beer; transporting coal in this manner was no easy task for people or animals. Roy looked forward to stroking the mule he had befriended, once they stopped. As they took the bend, the mule stumbled and fell into the canal. Several men and boys, watching from the pub benches, ran and jumped into the canal to rescue it.

Without a thought for his own safety, Roy jumped in. It was lucky that there were others there as Roy was only able to doggy paddle around. The mule was dragged out safely and rubbed down with a towel, then Rose asked for:

' …a round of applause for young Roy.'

She had observed the family's attempts to get him to swim. Her husband Joe had never learnt, even though he had spent his life, living and working on narrowboats. Beaming, dripping, Roy had found his courage. Like many, he had found that love for another is the greatest opponent of fear.

Rose told his mother that they were looking for a buyer for this mule. Eagerly Roy said that he knew one. His mother looked at him puzzled. In his young life he had learnt another very useful lesson – '*grandmas* can't say **no**!'

Chapter 8.

IS ANYBODY THERE?

Like most boys, the Allen boys loved anything with a sense of danger and excitement. A favourite game was 'knock and run.' Daringly someone would knock on a door, then run away and hide as fast as they could. Friends watching from a bush, or behind one of the many hedges, would find it funny to see the adults coming to the door, confused or angry, looking for them. It was a bit like hide and seek but much more dangerous - so much more fun! Adults, tired from working long hours, would come out with big sticks and woe betide anyone who got caught.

Les Allen, 'Capel,' as he was known, was getting a lot of stick from some of the dominoes team at his local pub.

'I'm sure it's your lot doing it Capel. It's driving me mad. Every time I shut me eyes the bloody door goes. I don't care who they are. When I catch 'em I'm really gonna let' em ave it!'

Well, Capel didn't want his kids hurt. He sympathised that they needed a bit of fun before blackout and toys were in very short supply; they hadn't even got a football thanks to the war. Even so he didn't want to look as if he couldn't control his own children and lose face down the pub and he certainly didn't want the children hurt.

He lined them up - Roy, 4, Don, 8 and Les 12. They looked so innocent. But he figured that they were involved in the door knocking, because *he'd* had no knocks on *his* door. He gave them a good talking to. If they got caught at knock and run they'd feel the end of *his* strap as well. They all nodded obediently.

But he'd mistakenly only said: '*if* they got caught!'

Well, after a bit of thought, they came up with an ingenious idea. A long length of string and some blocks of wood and nobody had to knock on the door; you could pull the string from quite a distance in a good hiding place. Nobody'd stand a chance of catching you, or knowing who'd pulled the string. It took quite a bit of setting up, but it was even more brilliant because you could knock on a lot of doors at the same time and watch all the angry men in their dressing gowns and ladies in their curlers, all running out together, with sticks and rolling pins, shouting.

Well, even more complaints. This time to Maud. She stuck up for her children, lying that they were in home at that time; but what with the war, five children and the complaints and having to be strong for everyone, she felt she needed a pick me up. She decided to go to church on Sunday. She mentioned it to her friend Mary, who eagerly responded:

'I've heard they're having a new medium at the spiritualist church in Beduth on Sunday. Let's go and have a nice day out. Shall I ask a few more friends?'

'Yes, it'll do us all good to have a day out,' Maud agreed.

Sunday morning, she put on her best dress and got her best hat and gloves out of the archives, really looking forward to a few hours without her family. Les, and Don were instructed to mind Roy.

The group of women set off happily.

It was beautiful inside the chapel, with flowers everywhere and so peaceful. You could totally forget the problems of the outside world. It was extremely popular in the war years with death and uncertainty being daily acquaintances.

At home, however, young Les was having problems. Roy wasn't used to his mother not being in the house and was having a paddy. He wondered if she would come back. He kept hearing adults talk of people dying and disappearing.

'Look be good and I'll show you where she is. We can walk back with her when it's finished,' Les comforted.

The three boys set off. They arrived at the chapel. The doors were shut. Roy still wasn't happy. The large stone building with its high wooden doors looked a frightening place, like a castle or a prison. Was his mum shut in there?

'Nobody's shut in. It's nice in there. They all

sing and stuff,' Les tried to reassure but had heard that people tried to get in touch with the dead.

'Shall we have a quick look Les?' Don was curious.

They all were. They opened the doors, just enough for all three of them to peer in; Les's head at the top, then Don's, then Roy at the bottom kneeling on the floor.

The new medium at the front of the chapel was hoping to make a good impression. Everyone sat there a little bit frightened, and apprehensive, wondering if they would personally get a message from the deceased.

'... Is anybody there?.......... Is anybody there?' wailed the medium. Her voice echoing creepily round the stone walls of the church. Les and Don were mesmerised. Eyes like saucers. The medium continued, excitedly raising her voice:

'... I can see someone. Yes, I can see someone from spirit world. It's a child.....with blonde curly hair and.... blue eyes. Does that mean anything to you?' The lady she was addressing nodded.

It was indeed a child. Roy had crawled under and popped his head up over the back of the wooden church seat. Not seeing his mum, he crawled along and popped up again, looking over someone else's shoulder.

'… No, no it's faded… The spirit's with the lady over there in the red dress.'

'Don, go 'n get him back!' Les whispered loudly. Don crawled in and popped his head up, looking to see where Roy was now.

'…There's an older boy, in a grey cap,' said the medium.

Mary's friend, sitting between Maud and Mary whispered proudly:

'I've got psychic powers I can see them!'

They all looked. Maud's face went red. Mary held her hands over her mouth trying not to laugh too loudly. Don and Roy kept popping up all over the chapel, as Don tried to catch Roy. More and more of the congregation started laughing as they realized what was happening. Don grabbed Roy and on hands and knees pulled him along the floor and out the door. They all scarpered.

Capel came home from the pub. They'd gone too far this time. He was not going to be the laughing stock of the pub. Word of the chapel fiasco had got around. They needed to be disciplined.

'Don't hit them!' Maud pleaded. Capel took his belt off. He looked at his three sons, eyes like frightened rabbits. It was his proper duty as a father to discipline them. Eventually, he spoke firmly:

'You're all grounded until further notice!' Everyone sighed with relief. '*And* you're to sit *quietly* and not move!'

Well for boys, this was a worse punishment than a beating that would have hurt like hell but been quickly over. Just sitting there, night after night, after a boring day at school, watching their dad snoring in a chair. It was worse knowing that all the other children were running free in the fresh air. Capel was just glad he'd got the respect back at the pub. The boys couldn't see it ending. Their resentment of him reached an all- time high. They thought they'd have a bit of fun.

They'd found a wig. It was from a doll. Sadly, treasured doll's heads smashed if they were dropped on concrete so if played with often didn't last long. They waited until their dad's snoring had reached a crescendo and, hands shaking, glued the long blonde ringlets, with a nice big pink ribbon on top, to his half-bald head. They sat there giggling, but then, as time rolled on, they thought about what they had done and started to get scared. On cue, usual time, Capel awoke. The boys felt really scared now and wished they hadn't done it. Their father walked over to the mantelpiece for his pipe, and caught sight of his reflection in the mirror. He laughed out loud. A real hearty laugh. They all joined in nervously, very relieved. Their father picked up a lipstick from the shelf, coloured his nose red, some red circles on his cheeks and red eyebrows then danced around in his string vest, his fat belly wobbling making them all laugh. He was still very merry from the beer he'd had earlier.

'Well, I s'pose I'd better get ready for work,' he said. He was on the night shift at the nearby munitions factory. He went off to his bedroom. They heard a loud:

'Aaaargh, I'll kill the little bl***ers,' as he couldn't pull the wig off.

He ran downstairs. No sign of them! He ran outside, grabbed a shovel and ran down the street. Well, if you want to be taken seriously in the community, running down the street in a vest, fat belly wobbling, a clown face, blonde ringlets and a shovel in your hand, is not the thing to do. The group of women nattering outside the shop, and the group of men coming out of his local, wondered if someone had escaped from the asylum.

The boys decided to stay at their uncles until it was safe to come home. Capel was so angry. It looked as if he couldn't control his own children.

However, naughty as they were, he soon missed them; the house was just too quiet without them. Maud went all the way up to Bedworth town and bought him a trilby hat on credit to hide his sore head. He looked in the mirror. He looked very distinguished.

'You look like Churchill,' Maud's friend, Mary remarked. Pride healed, he was back to his old self.

'That nice butcher up town sold us a pig's bladder for the boys as well. That should help keep them out of mischief.' Maud had her fingers crossed.

'Well, I s'pose I'd better go and get the three musketeers back home,' Capel said beaming.

The boys were really excited as Maud washed the pig's bladder under the tap from the rainwater tank. The other tap was for drinking only. She showed them how to blow it up and tie it to make a football. Eagerly they went out to play. All the children in their street and the next turned up for a game – that is all except Jim, Roy's best friend. Roy ran round the corner to Jim's house to get him. His mother answered the door, a pretty woman in her time but now showing the wear and tear of years of hardship.

'He's not coming out cos he's got no shoes,' she said.' He's been out the last few days without any but he's cut his feet so I'm making him stay in till it heals a bit.'

Maud, rinsing clothes in the sink, was surprised to see Roy return home, heavy with worry.

'Whatever's the matter, our Roy? Why aren't you out playing? Everyone's having a great time!'

'Me shoes are hurting me mam,' he said quietly.

She didn't think they'd last much longer. They'd been repaired and had cardboard put in to cover the latest hole. Roy wasn't one to complain and loved football so they must be really hurting. She really didn't want him to miss out on the football - pig's bladders didn't last forever! She had the difficult job of stretching the family finances. She often thought of Jesus with the few loaves and fishes and large crowd to feed. Resourcefully, she paid weekly into an account at a large store in town and when the bill came down she could have more credit. She sighed and dried her hands on her pinny. Taking it off, she said:

'Do you think your feet can manage to walk up to Bedworth for some new boots?'

Would they! He hadn't had *new* boots before.

Well, Maud was surprised at how well he did walk up to the department store considering he'd limped into the kitchen with his sad tale. Then, when measured in the shop, his feet hadn't grown much. She didn't say anything though. They were here now; his shoes had just about had it and being the youngest of three boys, he had all hand me downs, rarely anything new. His face was a picture of ecstasy as he tried on the pair of brand new boots.

'Shall I throw away the old ones. Madam?' asked the very correct shop assistant. Maud nodded, they'd had their day.

'No!' shouted Roy. Well, what a disturbed reaction. Maud knew something wasn't quite right.

'Roy you'd better explain yourself! Right

now!' she said in a tone not to be argued with.

'They're for Jim. He hasn't been out all week and doesn't know when he'll get some shoes.'

Roy hung his head, ashamed at not being totally honest with his mother.

'Poor Jim', she thought. She well remembered times without shoes from her own childhood. Some of the local children were really suffering. Only the week earlier, she had gone with her children and all the neighbours to a house in the next street to pay her respects. Wistfully, she remembered the beautiful little face of the thin, small child laid out on the kitchen table, dead from consumption. Well, they really couldn't afford it, but there was only one thing to do:

'We'll have another pair please. Roy, what size-are his feet the same size as yours?'

Roy arrived at Jim's house.

'Can I come in and see Jim, please Mrs Blake?'... 'I've got something for him,' he added proudly. She supposed it was another bird's egg. The two boys spent long happy days nesting. They loved the birds, and were learning all the different varieties and their songs and habits. Young as they were, they could already climb fairly high trees, only ever carefully taking one egg, then shinning back down the tree with the egg in their mouth to keep it safe. A pin prick, to make a hole and carefully suck out the interior, then their egg would be ready to add to the prized collection. Jim thought the same as his mother.

'That's a good box you've got, Roy, and tissue paper,' Jim was impressed. Then, noticing Roy's new boots his voice dipped enviously 'and you've got new boots, they're nice,' he said quietly. Roy was grinning from ear to ear.

'Well open the tissue paper then - they're yours, me mams bought them!' Jim was … totally speechless! His mother quickly wiped away her tears with her pinny.

Capel was also delighted with Maud's present. He put his smartest suit on, then his trilby hat. Feeling very distinguished he set off to join his domino team.

Dozens of children were playing ball with the pig's bladder outside his front gate. They paused for him to pass and chorused :

'Hello Mr Allen.'

He seemed to be getting his due respect at last. The street kids *were* learning to love and respect this man who always made time for them and helped mend their bikes - but the temptation was just too irresistible for one young lad.

Klonk! The makeshift football hit Capel's new hat from behind, and knocked it off his head. He angrily picked it up from the road and turned, like a bear with a sore head, to give them a piece of his mind........ But of course - there wasn't anybody there!

Chapter 9.

SINGING THE SAME TUNE!

War or no war, the Blackhorse Road community were determined to have some fun. Even more so because of the war. The climate of living with fear and sleepless, terrifying nights made every day of being alive and free extra precious. At every opportunity people got together socially. These social events were easy to arrange. Neighbours popped into one another's houses. The local shop and 'Boat' pub were regular meeting places. The quickest form of communication though, was over the garden fences. Messages and gossip jumped over the garden fences and hedges like racehorses on a steeplechase.

Like all news, the message facts sometimes got smudged. It was sadly reported that 'old gal Groves' was on her last legs. She came from an established, poor family in the community. When the news came of her passing away, two familiar elderly women went round the community collecting for the family.

Everyone gave what they could, even the local factory. The ladies arrived sombrely at the house, well pleased with the collection. They were startled when the door was answered by – old gal Groves herself! Completely at a loss to know what to do or say… they just handed over the money to the toothless, smiling old woman.

Maud Allen became a very enthusiastic organiser; she arranged regular coach trips. People paid towards them over a few weeks, then families went to other pubs and villages, parks, amusement parks – anywhere people suggested. They took cricket bats for the men and alcohol and all sang heartily on the coaches: 'Roll out the barrel';'Run rabbit run'; 'Hitler's only got one ball.'

It was something for everyone to look forward to. In between these trips groups of women and children would have days out, walks in the country all together, blackberry picking, picnics, swimming in the rivers and canals. Many summer evenings were spent on a bit of waste ground adjacent to the street. People would bring wooden boxes to sit on and their own home-made alcohol and pop and someone would bring a gramophone. Quite a large crowd would gather. The local pub also had regular sing-along nights. Someone would stand up and start singing and everyone would join in.

Occasionally, local businesses would arrange sporting events. One particularly unforgettable cricket match was arranged by a Bayton Road factory – manual workers against the management and office workers. All the community turned up to watch. The manual workers went to the local pub first; then with everyone else from the pub, followed by women and children, merrily made their way to the cricket field.

They were dressed just in their ordinary clothes; it was all they had with clothing being rationed. The bosses' team came out, cheered by their wives and children. Then, last came the factory owner – dressed all in dazzling white, proper cricket gear. Being the only one all in 'proper' gear, he really stood out from the crowd. It was not only clothes that were in short supply; the cricket field was kindly borrowed from a farm. It was a good match. The watching crowd cheered and clapped and shouted heartily. Everyone played their best. The jubilant crowd all agreed that the highlight of the match was the boss's performance. He really tried his utmost to show that he was the best there. Running to catch a ball in his dazzling whites, he slipped on a large sloppy cow pat, his head landing in another; everyone roared with laughter. What a great day!

The local vicar got to hear of Maud Allen's organising abilities. He was on a difficult mission. He wanted to help the German prisoners of war, who had a camp nearby. He thought he'd try and get families in the community to invite them to dinner. So far he'd had nothing but looks of horror and disbelief and doors practically slammed in his face but he wasn't one to give in without a fight.

Timidly he knocked on the Allen's door. Maud opened the door.

'I already know what you've come for, vicar,' she said. News had travelled over the back garden fences quicker than he could get round the streets. 'You know what you can do with that idea,' she continued indignantly: 'After what they've done to us. They wouldn't be here if they hadn't come to **bomb** us ….. And nobody round here would speak to us.'

He nodded understandingly while she continued:

'And they don't seem to have it that bad. I've seen 'em - out in the fields digging ditches while our men are away getting killed or doing twelve hour shifts in the factories and down the pits, then spending nights doing ARP.' She was amazed that he had the guile to ask her to have the *enemy*, the people who were *bombing them* - to *dinner*! The three boys had joined her, not wanting to miss anything.

'What beautiful children you have Mrs Allen. They'd look marvelous in my choir.'

Maud beamed. She was very proud of them.

'They're not the best of singers,' she said.

'Oh that wouldn't be a problem, they could just stand at the front. They're like cherubs.'

'Thank you vicar, not many people call them

110

that,' she laughed, 'But I'm afraid they're joining a boxing club on Sundays.'

'Well if you change your mind, we'd love to have them in church…….. You know the war prisoners aren't having it that great. They don't know if their families are alive or dead!'

Maud shook her head and closed the door. It wasn't her fault – she hadn't started the *bloody* war!

Boxing clubs – that was the answer. What a great idea to get more youngsters into church. The vicar was excited. He'd learnt to box in his younger days – he'd been quite good. If he hadn't had his calling who knows he might have been a boxing champ. Walking down the dirt track along by the field, he glanced around – no one in sight. He gave a right punch, then a few left jabs, some nifty footwork. Yes he hadn't lost it – he ducked to avoid the punch of his invisible opponent. Lost in his dream world, he didn't see the enthralled youngsters sitting up in the trees.

Maud didn't sleep well. She just couldn't get it out of her head: 'They don't know if their families are alive or dead.' She couldn't think of anything worse. Still, she had to cheer up; today a group of women and children were all going on a nice picnic over by the farm pond, just along the canal and a few fields away. It was a lovely day. The hedges were embroidered with pink and white dog roses; the fields a patchwork of colour and texture. The women all chatted away happily:

'Did you hear about Mrs Smith's geese?' someone asked. 'She threw out the dregs of her home-made sloe gin – it must have been really strong! The geese lay on the floor, dead, after drinking it..... So, she plucked them all before she went to bed. I think she must av bin *really* drunk. When she got up the next morning the three geese were waddling around – with NO FEATHERS!'

Everyone laughed.

'Oh dear - the poor geese!'

'They're okay; she's knitted them all little jackets to keep them warm.'

They passed the POW's in the field. Everyone had a good look.

'They don't look nasty, do they?' someone said.

'No,' said Maud, 'Some of' 'em are only boys.' She continued wistfully: 'The vicar said they don't know if their families are alive or dead!'

They all looked at the prisoners then at their own children skipping along and laughing. The party was suddenly much more sombre. Someone piped up:

'Well, it's not our bloody fault is it?'

'No. It's not,' agreed Maud. But it's probably not theirs either......It's governments that make wars. And stupid dictators.' They all nodded. 'Do you remember the last war? We had a right load of donkeys in charge. If you didn't charge when they said, you got shot for disobeying. Well I expect it's the same for them.'

'Yes, it looks like they've got a right clown in charge,' added another lady. 'I've seen him at the cinema in the Charlie Chaplain film.' They all laughed at the thought of the humorous portrayal of Hitler. It

113

was good that they could laugh at the Fuhrer who was attacking Europe like a rabid dog.

'When they come to dinner, they bring you presents,' a quiet member of the group piped up. They all looked at her suspiciously. ... 'Or so the vicar says.' She wasn't that brave! Well towards the end of the afternoon they had decided that if anyone from their little group invited the Jerries for dinner, they wouldn't be 'sent to Coventry,' though they might still face a lot of animosity from others!

Maud relaxed and enjoyed the day out but when she got home, she wondered if she'd done the right thing. Well it was done now, no going back, but how on earth would she tell the old man, Capel?

She never did quite find the moment or the courage to tell him, so arranged the meal event for when he was at work.

As the big day grew nearer, she seriously doubted that she had done the right thing. No husband there – with prisoners of war – Jerries – the ENEMY. They looked pretty harmless in the fields; they weren't even guarded very closely, but what if they did try and escape from her house; maybe take someone hostage, using a kitchen knife. Her imagination ran riot. She should have told her husband. She decided that there was no going back- but she better not risk the children. She decided to ask two supportive friends so that she was not on her own. They were naturally nosey and eagerly agreed to come. She told the children to all go out and explained why. The girls had already got other arrangements anyway; they had busy social lives. The boys didn't argue. They could tell by her decisive tone that it was pointless. They discussed it out in the street with their friends.

'What, you mam'n her friends having Jerries for dinner. I bet you're glad you're going out. I don't expect they'll taste very nice.'

'No dickhead, we're not bloody cannybulls - they're coming to eat dinner – mam's best rabbit stew.'

'What – JERRIES and nobody there to save your mam?' Their friend voiced their concerns. They hatched a plan.

Maud, Ida and Polly wore their best floral dresses and put some flowers on the table. They'd got a gramophone to put some music on because they didn't know if the Germans would be able to say much so didn't quite know how to make them welcome. They'd never met anyone from another country before. The visitors arrived. Two men, Hubert in his forty's and Adolf just nineteen years old. Only Adolf didn't tell them his proper name at first, said it was 'Hans'. The men were more nervous than the women and felt a bit safer coming in pairs. They were treated okay in the prison barracks but feared that without guards the local people might blame them personally for the war and vent their anger on them. They were clearly very moved by the warm welcome that they received. They ate enthusiastically. After the meal, they brought out pictures of their families, whose fate they didn't know. They heard of bombings on their country *more* destructive than the Coventry blitz. Evil was proving to be very infectious!

'You very nice people,' said Hubert 'Why you
116

bomb us? We no want war with you.'

'**No! You...** bombed ... **us**,' replied Ida, loudly and slowly.

'No, we *no* want war with you!' The women found this very strange. Maud decided to change the subject quickly:

'Would you like to try my elderberry wine?'

And the guests had brought presents. They were very good at making things. There were slippers for Maud and Capel, and a wooden pipe. Wow, was Maud relieved. She knew that Capel would find out and this would help a lot. They hadn't had slippers for years and Capel loved to smoke a pipe. Tobacco was one of the few things encouraged to boost moral by the government and not rationed. The POW's had also saved all their fat rations and eggs from the prison fowl and made a beautiful cake. POW's got more rations than civilians. They got the same as the armed forces. Cake was a rare wartime treat for the Allen family. The guests had also carved, out of wood from tree branches, a kind of flute.

'For your children,' Hans said 'I give?' He walked over towards the settee. Unbeknown to Maud the three boys were sitting behind the settee and couldn't resist keep popping up to have a look. They had decided that their mum needed protection and were sitting there with pen knives, a catapult and – a *gun* that one of their gang had borrowed for them.

Maud was embarrassed. Those children!

'Let's have some music on. Put the music on!' Oh no, she wished young Les hadn't chosen *that* song. It was a popular war song. It was hard not to keep mentioning the war especially since one of them had confessed that his name was Adolf. Once or twice she had unintentionally called Hubert, 'Uboat.' She really liked them and didn't want to make them feel uncomfortable. The popular record sang out: 'Underneath the lantern by the barracks gate……..The song: 'Lili Marlene.'

'I know this song,' said Hubert. 'It is the song we sing as we go off to battle.'

'*No,* ' said Ida, It's the song *our* troops sing as *they*

118

go into battle.' The two sides looked at each other dumbfounded. Both sides went to fight each other singing the same song. How futile it made war seem. They all started singing it in their own languages. Both sides trying to sing it louder. Young Roy very untunefully, playing the wooden flute, using just one note like a kazoo.

The afternoon had been a great success and the guests went back to the prison barracks really happy.

'What was your family like?' asked Adolf's friend.

'Very hospitable,' he replied, 'very kind and friendly, but not very musical. I would rather face their spitfires than their singing,' he laughed.

The visit was followed by more. One of the many presents from the visitors, treasured as a memory of that special first day, was a wooden ornament that Hubert had carved himself of Lili Marlene underneath the lantern with her lover. And their hosts repaid them with their kindest hospitality and........a lot more singing!

The boys returned the gun to their friend:

'Did you manage to shoot any of 'em?' he asked eagerly.

'No, they were really *friendly*. It's a bit hard to have a good conversation with 'em though; they talk about dankeys, every time you speak to them and I don't know what that is, must be summat german.'

'Sound a strange lot to me,' said their friend, taking his catapult and gun and carefully putting them in his school pump bag.

***

Capel arrived home from work quite merry. He had felt that he needed a detour at the pub first. Maud looked anxious.

'I **know**!' he said.

Clocking on at work, one of his colleagues had said to him:

'Our Emily's having jerries for dinner today.'

'Phew,' said Capel, 'I couldn't see my missus doing that.' The look from all the others told him that he was the last to know. He wasn't very pleased about that, but work and the pub had worked off his anger and he thought Maud probably knew best. She always did. She showed him his slippers and pipe.

'Well, bloody Norah!' he exclaimed.

'Dad who's Norah – you know bloody Norah. Is it Norah from the shop?' A curious young voice asked.

'A man just wants his snap and peace and quiet when he comes home – not bloody stupid questions.'

He sat down at the dinner table and picked up his knife and fork. On cue Maud brought his dinner in. It was smaller than usual – she'd had to stretch it a lot today. But they'd saved half the cake – a massive piece for him.

'Adolf and Uboat brought it for you,' she said. His eyebrows raised at the names.

'Well, bloody Norah!'

He finished his meal and tried out his new pipe and slippers.

'When they come again, hi want to be 'ere, so hi can learn 'em how to play dominoes, hic!'

The next Sunday the church was unusually full. The vicar was feeling extremely proud. He wondered if it was his community organising, the POW meals or his boxing club.

In fact the message that had galloped over the garden fences faster than a racehorse at Aintree, was that the vicar danced along boxing imaginary foe, and everyone wanted to see for themselves if he had *really* gone…. 'stark raving mad!'

Chapter 10.

THE MAGNIFICENT SIX!

Although Don loved his kid brother and let him tag along most of the time, he occasionally liked to escape with his friends. He cantered up the side of their home, proudly, on a beautiful honey and cream coloured palomino pony that he had borrowed for the day. His mate followed on a bigger, statuesque horse. Roy was really impressed, he loved horses. These were awesome.

'You can hold the reins, Roy, while I get us some food and drink out of the house, we'll probably be gone all day.' Don was elated.

'Let me come, Don, *please!' Roy begged.*

'I can't Roy you haven't got a horse.'

His friend chuckled.

'I can sit on the back of you. I'll hold on tight!'

'I would Roy but the palominos not built for two, not to go fast; we're going to be galloping all round Beduth.'

Roy eyed the palomino, she was beautiful, but It was true, she wasn't very big for a pony.

'…so if I had a horse?'

'Yeah course mate, but you haven't!'

'You hold the reins! I'm going to get one.… I'll be quick!'

Don's friend was eager to go:

'Let's go, Don - where's he going to get a horse from, and how could he keep up with us?'

'Oh he can ride alright, but God knows where he'll get a horse – we can wait a bit while we make some sandwiches.' Don knew that Roy had learnt to ride his uncle's small pony almost as soon as he could walk. They had put the cute pair in a show at Bedworth Oval. Then he had spotted Roy and his mates when he walked past a farmer's field. Without permission, they were riding the horses bare-back around the field.

Roy's mission didn't take long. His grandma Wilson lived in a cottage just up the road and he'd already learnt that grandmas don't know how to say 'no'. She had an equine friend that pulled her little shopping cart occasionally. She had been persuaded by Roy to buy it from The Skinners, and Roy had suddenly became a very regular visitor, helping care for 'Joey.' Not that he needed much care. Joey's life was now luxury compared to pulling a narrowboat of coal along a canal towpath in all weathers; a very hard life for the people as well. And he cost so little to keep. He lived in a little shed at the bottom of the garden and at night went a walk and returned in the morning, well grazed.

Don and his friend had to laugh when Roy and his mule appeared.

'You, won't keep up with us on a stupid donkey,' Don's mate sniggered. His arrogant horse joined in with a snort and held his head up arrogantly, his proud mane flowing.

They all looked at Joey's short thick head, short mane and long donkeyish ears.

'He's not a donkey, he's a mule and he's not stupid. He'll beat your horse,' Roy replied challengingly. Joey joined in. He whinnied like a horse, then flicked up his back legs, kicking the large horse and letting out a loud donkey 'EEEEEE-ORE!'

Joey was not to be sneered at; mules, the offspring of a male donkey and a female horse, were often chosen to pull the heavy boat loads because they were considered more patient and sure-footed than a horse, and faster, less obstinate and more intelligent than a donkey.

'Alright, alright you've both made your point,' Don was trying hard not to laugh, 'I'll get the saddle out of the shed.'

The brothers were gutted to find the once beautiful, treasured, leather saddle had been shredded.

'That must be what dad used to mend our shoes,' Don saw Roy's upset face – 'he wouldn't have done it if he'd had a choice Roy, we have to have shoes.'

The friend spoke:

'Well that's that then, let's go Don, we can't mess about *all* day.'

Roy looked at him defiantly, picked up a coal sack, threw it over the back of the mule, stood on an upturned coal bucket and climbed on.

'Yes, let's go, cowboy's,' he whooped!

Well, the procession no longer looked so grand, but the elder boy's had to admire the plucky pair, though they doubted that they'd keep up for long.

Again they underestimated. Roy and Joey kept up with them as they rode all the way up to Bedworth and whooping excitedly, galloped round the town centre, then on to Bulkington and a circular ride back. Eventually, late evening they returned to Blackhorse Road, elated.

They stopped outside Grandma Wilson's cottage to

return Joey.

'Oh that was brill,' enthused Roy as he climbed off his trusty steed, 'Like being *real* cowboys!'

'You certainly walk like one,' Don laughed. 'Have you poo'd in your pants?'

Roy hadn't soiled his pants, but his legs were injured; they were bracket shaped; the coarse sacking had rubbed all the skin off his inside legs.

'Oooh,' he groaned....... It was worth it though, weren't it Joey?'

Joey had never had such a great adventure. He listened attentively as Roy spoke:

'I'll be able to com'n see you a lot this week, mate; I should manage to swing at least a week off school with these legs,' he laughed through the pain.

Chapter 11

FRIENDS AND FOE!

Exhall primary school in Bedworth was in need of repair and it was decided that the boys in Roy's class would have to be sent elsewhere whilst their classroom was renovated. A makeshift classroom was found in nearby Longford, in a chapel at the end of Lady Lane. Roy Allen had seen how his brother Les had been bullied as a child when he ventured over the bridge into Longford, but Roy wasn't worried as he set off. Les was now a local boxing celebrity and, with everyone wanting to say that they had beat Les Allen's brother, Roy had had to learn to fight for survival. After sparring with his elder brothers, his own boxing skills were well developed and his success in fighting in self-defence at his primary school had added to his esteem. He was now considered to be the 'cock' of the school and had a bit of the cockiness that went with the title.

He lined up with his classmates outside the chapel that was to be their temporary classroom. They were now ten and eleven years old, the year before high school; still in short trousers but feeling quite big for their boots, as they were now the eldest at primary school and had won the area football cup.

The Longford children turned up to stare at them curiously. Feeling brave due to being in a large crowd, the Longforders started to chant the local song about Bedworth:

'Strong in the arm, weak in the head, Beduth born and Beduth bred.'

'Come over here and say that, if you dare!' Some of the Bedworth lot had got their fists up ready. But they all had school and didn't want caning. The Longford ring leader had the answer:

'Your best fighter against ours; over the fields behind the chapel after school!'

'You're on you've got no chance – we've got Les Allen's brother!'

'Oh no, here we go again,' Roy's heart sank. With friends like his who needed enemies.

It was impossible to concentrate on the days lessons. His class mates were all excited about the after-school entertainment.

'Give it to 'em good and proper Ruey. They won't mess with us agen, we'll show em.'

We? Roy wished it was 'we.' Still none of the Longforders had looked too tough. He'd have to go through with it; maybe a few good punches and they'd leave him in peace.

The hands of the classroom clock seemed to whizz round, pushed by the will of his classmates. Once outside their animal excitement erupted. Violence was widely accepted and commonplace in the years following the wars. 'We will fight them on the beaches.....we will never surrender!' this was a generation that had been educated by these speeches.

'Might is right,' existed in many classrooms and homes, with canings and belts to discipline children. To watch someone fighting back whilst they themselves remained safe appealed to many.

Roy trooped over to the chosen field, spurred on by the enthusiasm of his supporters. A large crowd of children of all ages had gathered there - a savage army of small spectators. Their champion stood out in front of them.

Roy's army all froze like statues. Roy's legs turned to jelly. He gulped in disbelief as he looked upwards at large tanned muscles, wild raven hair and black stone eyes. Looking just slightly down from eye level Roy could see the stomach that he would be able to reach to punch – strong muscular brown tough, rippling leather. He gulped again. One of his friends voiced his thoughts:

'He's never at your school, that's cheating. He's a man!'

'He *is* at our school,' smirked a small weasel faced Longforder. 'Fury's a gypsy. He's staying at our school till his reading and writing's good enough for high school. He's a champion bare-knuckle fighter. They fight to the death!'

Fury was only a few years older than Roy but had undergone the adolescent metamorphosis that catapults boys into manhood. He was now a strong, very muscular man.

The crowd circled round David and Goliath excitedly, a pack of wild animals, baying for blood. White faced, Roy held up his two fists, trying to shield his head professionally, praying that he would come out of it alive. He soldiered on in the noise of the battlefield as his body was pounded again and again with painful blows. His head was going fuzzy, his opponent blurry. He forced a weak punch back. His colossal opponent let out a loud 'Aaaaaaagh!' and stepped well back. Just about focusing, Roy saw a small dark- haired woman bashing a broom on Fury's head. She grabbed Fury by the hair and shouted something incomprehensible at him before herding him away with hard wacks of the broom.

***

Two arms entwined Roy's; one each side, giving his jellied legs much needed support. He was too weak and giddy to resist. Two women guided him to the next field towards the gypsy encampment.

His classmates were genuinely worried now. They watched as travellers and fierce, yapping dogs appeared from the circle of caravans that Roy was being escorted into:

'I bet they'll put a curse on him.'

'Or eat him.' They looked at one another and, like a stampede of cattle, ran away as fast as their legs would carry them.

A small group of the more conscientious ran breathlessly several miles to Roy's house. They were disappointed by his mother's response. Instead of organising a cavalry to save her son she assured them that he was 'in good hands.'

Maud had good reason to trust the gypsies. As a small child her eyes had been very badly ulcerated. Her parents feared that she would go blind but could not afford a doctor. In desperation they took the medical advice of a gypsy who told them to gather snails and crush them, then smear the paste on little Maud's eyes. Her eyes healed and she firmly believed that it was this treatment that saved her from a possible life of blindness. There is something in the silvery secretion of a snail that enables the soft creature to glide on sharp surfaces and not get lacerated.

Roy was a bit apprehensive as he was firmly walked into the gypsy encampment. He knew of his mother's respect for the Romany people but had also heard the scaremongering of others who called them 'dirty gypos.' He had just been battered by one and didn't know whether his treatment would be hostile because he'd been the enemy fighter. Still, feeling a bit concussed, with jelly legs he hadn't got it in him to break free from the two gripping arms and run. He was very relieved when the two women said something he could understand:

'We'll gets you all cleaned up n' a noice drink. We'll gets yous as good as new, now dun't yous worry dearie.'

He managed to focus on a brown, wooden looking

135

caravan. He thought of his own home, a large four bedroomed council house. This didn't look much bigger than his coal bunker and it was the same corrugated, overturned barrel shape. How on earth did large families live in them? Wooden steps led up to the upside down horseshoe shaped front opening, artistically painted with bright flowers and exotic birds.

'Av lad, gets yous up in the vargo. We needs to wash theys cuts n' bruises n' gets yous a noice drink.'

Crikey they were actually taking him in. Curiosity and thirst won and he let himself be helped up inside. He didn't know any non-gypsy who'd actually been inside a caravan.

Roy's mouth opened wide in amazement at the sight before him - like Aladdin entering the cave of glittering treasure. Crystal glass and mirrored doors sparkled. Pictured plates rimmed with gold hung from the walls. He wondered if this was a special gypsy palace. He had only seen such dazzling opulence in books. Catching his reflection in a mirror he felt too dirty to be in there. Indeed he was privileged. Many of the 'dirty' gypsies as he had heard them called thought that most non-gypsies or 'gadges' weren't up to their standards of cleanliness. The mistrust was mutual. He obeyed and watched speechless as he was told to:

'Sit thee down ere lad,' in a comfy chair by a small warm cast iron stove. A clean cup was washed again in a bowl and filled with cordial with a tot of whisky, then a different bowl and white cloths for bathing his wounds, then a different bowl and carbolic soap for washing the cloths. How they managed such comfort and hospital hygiene in such confined space had to be seen to be believed. His mother had indeed been right to advise him not to pay too much heed to what people say and make his own judgement. Never again would he succumb to prejudice.

After a huge bowl of rabbit stew, he was helped into a trap pulled by a pony with jigsaw markings and brightly coloured ribbons and waved off by a crowd of people and interested dogs, like he was royalty. A kindly looking old man with a creased leprechaun face wearing a trilby was instructed to:

'tek im um to Blackhoss road. E's one of Maudey Wilson's lads, whos married Capel Allen. E's a good un young Ruey is.'

***

'Ruey' was now his nick- name. It had been shortened from 'Rooster,' endowed on him because of his love of getting up early with the cockerels. The dawn chorus, missed by most slumbering bodies is the best time of day. His father, 'Capel' had thus educated him. Together they revelled in the morning orchestra of birdsong, as the birds joyously greet each new day. It was time enjoyed with his dad. Like most men, Capel's role was the breadwinner of the family: working long hours, followed by leisure time at his local 'The Old Boat,' mostly playing dominoes with a few pints of 'rough'. On returning home, before his dinner and sleep, he would be merrily tipsy and sometimes make the family laugh, especially with his antics with the ferrets that they kept for rabbiting. Cute looking, wide-eyed, furry creatures, with small ears and a small sensitive, whiskered nose that twitched inquisitively. However, their innocent faces hid sharp, fang like teeth and a bravery and fierceness that enabled them to go down tunnels in search of rabbits and rats. They loved tunnels of any kind. Capel (tipsily) would put one by the opening of his trouser leg and let it run up to the top. If the ferret decided to bite it could have been very nasty. Ferrets lock their sharp, pointed teeth in and can rip flesh. They have strong jaws and are almost impossible to prise off. They also emit a foul pong when frightened.

The children watched spellbound as Capel and the ferrets performed their circus tricks. Maud couldn't look. Luckily Capel and the ferrets were comfortable enough with one another to enjoy this game with no injury. The family loved these antics and if they had any requests got them in whilst Capel was still a bit tipsy and acquiescent.

'Dad, I'm old enough to go rabbiting now. Will you take me?' Roy pleaded successfully.

***

Capel and his son got up whilst still dark. Capel half wished he hadn't made the promise. Rabbiting was illegal. He couldn't go back on his word now though – Roy looked so excited and, during and after the war, meat had been really expensive; rabbiting helped the family survive; Roy needed to learn sometime. Some farmers turned a blind eye because the overabundant rabbit population was ruining their crops, but if they wanted to they could press poaching charges with very hefty fines and possible imprisonment. The risk added to the excitement. They went to the ferret pens in the garden:

'You can 'ave this one, mind you look after him.'

'What mine to keep? Wow, thanks dad.' He thought for a minute: All the girl ferrets were called 'Jill.' 'I'll call him Jack!'

Roy couldn't believe it. His dad had given him his prize hybrid polecat-ferret. Capel had never dared risk putting this one in his trousers. He was really proud of the handsome creature, goldish with flecks of white, a white bib and little white socks of fur; larger than the others and a bit fiercer, and less handleable, but an amazing rabbiter. It had never hurt anyone, but he sensed a wildness in it which came from the wild polecat part of it. It was stouter and slower than the ferrets. When ferrets catch the rabbits down the holes they often suck the blood and stay down there after their meal. The only way to get them out is to try to guess where they are and dig them out, but because 'Jack' was not so lean and quick, the rabbits would pop out into the awaiting nets before Jack could catch them. Armed with a torch, some nets, sacks, a cosh and Jack in a sandbag, excitedly they set off in the dark. Capel chose an area abounding with rabbits opposite the Boat Inn, just down the road. They set the nets over all the holes they could find on a rabbit warren.

'Make sure you cover all the holes. If Jack comes out an uncovered one we could lose him,' Capel instructed.

Holes secured, Roy took Jack out of his bag and held him near a rabbit hole. His whiskers twitched excitedly. He needed no instruction; he eagerly darted down the hole, looking for dinner. Capel showed Roy how to bump the rabbits that popped up, on the back of the head, or hold them by their long ears and one quick snap of the neck. Roy dearly loved animals, but had experienced dead rabbits all his life as a main diet. He was a bit hesitant at first but knew that being a man meant feeding everyone as a matter of survival. He got on with it, as humanely as possible, proud of their haul. Capel was equally proud of his son facing up to manly responsibilities so young.

'Roy! STOP!' Capel whispered urgently. He switched off the torch. He could hear voices. 'Drop the bag. RUN!'

The two would-be poachers ran through the dark, not stopping for breath until they were inside their front door. Just one word was spoken the rest of the night:

'Jack,' said Roy sadly.

***

Roy obeyed his father's advice the next day not to go near the scene of crime and went to school as usual, and got on with the day, quieter than usual. At dusk when ferrets liven up and like rabbits start wanting their dinner, he took the garden ferrets some bread and milk, sad that he hadn't got them rabbit, but more sad that Jack wasn't there.

He went back in the house. His budgie 'Joey' called out:

'Who's a cheeky b****** then? ' Normally this would have cheered him up. This budgie was lasting well. He'd had a few die, until someone advised him to make a cage from an orange box with mesh on.

Given time and kind patience, Joey was now talking really well. They were interrupted abruptly when a red-faced friend ran into the living room.

'You've got to come quick Roy. I think it's your ferret.'

Roy grabbed a sack and ran with him to.............the pub! An incredible sight met his eyes. It was Jack, but not the sweet, doe-eyed mischievous little Jack. Ferociously, the animal had hunched its back, fluffed out its tail. Its body hair was standing on end. With a fierce, rasping hissing sound and high pitched chattering, the demon was threatening a group of women and children in the corner; some standing frightened on chairs and tables. They knew its bite could be vicious.

Roy beamed with admiration at the antics of this small creature.

'It's alright. He's just frightened,' Roy reassured. He spoke gently to Jack: 'Come on old pal, it's okay, it's okay. I've come to take you home.'

Gradually, the creature shrank to his normal size and, still with frightened eyes, let Roy put a pub towel over him and place him, meekly into the sack – but oh, the unbearable stink; there never was a stink like it!

***

The danger of rabbiting added to the excitement for Roy and he was soon an experienced rabbiter, providing nourishing food for grateful mouths. He remembered the kindness of the gypsy folk. Although the caravan had sparkled his mother assured him that these treasures had been built up over the years instead of putting savings in banks, and, like most people, the gypsies were struggling and had been very kind feeding him. He decided to take them some rabbits as a thank you present.

As he approached the campsite a pack of small dogs, like Yorkshire terriers came yapping round his feet viciously. Roy was used to bigger dogs and was startled at the fierceness of these tiny guard dogs. A resident came quickly to the rescue and waved them off before they did any damage. Roy gulped as he looked up at Fury – his enemy. He needn't have worried though; Fury now smiled and greeted him.

'Phew that was close,' said Roy, 'they nearly had me!'

'Once they gets to knows yous yee'l be safe,' Fury reassured.

'I've brought some rabbits for the ladies who fed me.' said Roy : 'A thank you present.'

'It be no bother, we allus share,' said Fury. 'Av.' *(Come).*

He escorted Roy inside the ring of wagons. A crowd of mixed age people were all sitting outside round an open fire, like bonfire night. Some of the ladies were peeling vegetables, some whittling wooden pegs, men just smoking pipes or watching the flames. Roy had only intended to visit the one caravan and leave his gift but the whole community excitedly welcomed him. The young children touched him curiously and even the dogs were now friendly.

'I've just brought a few rabbits,' he said nervously. 'I caught them myself.'

An elderly, wrinkled woman, with a headscarf on, spoke:

'Aye Ruey we've eared yous got a homin ferret, that gus up the pub.'

They all laughed:

'It be real kind of ee Ruey, but yous don't av to we's av load o' they rabbits. Come av sum edgeog wiv us.'

Roy watched, fascinated, as clay was peeled off a hedgehog cooked in the embers of the open fire. The spikes came off easily with the clay. The meat was a bit like pork but sweeter. With roast potatoes and a tot of whisky in his cordial, sitting by the open fire Roy felt a warm glow inside as well as out.

They loved his story of the polecat ferret and had many tips on rabbiting, and where the best places were to not get caught.

'Can yous read, Ruey?' a man asked. 'Oi's got this ere newspaper but wiv all the voyaging we's had to do workin ere, workin there we's never got much schoolin.'

Roy was really glad that he could do something to return their kindness. They all gathered round, listening intensely while he read the news highlights to them. They had a wireless but the news in the 'News of the World' was a lot juicier and more shocking than the formal BBC news. As it started to get dark, Roy said his goodbyes and promised to return to read to them again.

'We'll pay ees ter read to us, we'll pay yous well,' they implored.

From time to time Roy returned to read to the travellers. They always had a whip round for him and were so eager to hear his stories. Sometimes his natural mischievousness took over and he would stop a story at an important point and say he'd had enough.'

'Go on, go on. More wonga , more wonga, giz im more wonga.' They would collect more money (wonga) to persuade him to finish the stories giving him well enough for a few trips to the cinema and sweets. Mischievously he sometimes added a few juicy bits to the stories to make them, in the eyes of a youngster, more interesting.

There was no fooling Rosa though. The old gypsy, with twinkling eyes spoke to him on his own on his way out.

'Yous can go a long way, and make a lot of

money telling theys stories,' she advised, 'I should knows, but bees careful who yous tell em to,' she winked.

'You read people's fortunes in a crystal ball don't you Rosa, would you read mine?' He gestured his money.

She laughed: Keep yours wonga, I already knows yours .'

'Will I be rich?' he asked.

'Yous will be very rich………in things that *really* matter. And……yous will marry a woman with red hair.'

What Rosa lacked in formal reading skills she made up for in reading people. She had well developed life skills in psychology. She had a great fondness for young Ruey and the little red headed girl who was kindly teaching young gypsy children to read in school. She had seen the way Shirley had run to summon help to save Roy in the fight and well knew the strong power of self- fulfilling prophecy.

Roy chuckled bashfully:

'Me – *married*?'

They laughed together.

Roy felt a bit guilty at his reading antics and as soon as some news cropped up that he thought the travellers would like to know about, he eagerly went back to the camp with a newspaper. The women loved the story that his mum had kept about the princess Elizabeth's wedding and how the war influenced the occasion even though it had ended. Especially the fact that even royalty had clothes rations. A person's clothes rations bought about one outfit a year, that's if you could afford it. The princess was sent over 100 clothing ration coupons from well-wishers towards the material for her bridal gown, and her Greek fiancé, Prince Philip, wasn't allowed to invite his three sisters because they had German connections by marriage.

Although the war had been over for several years, things were still very hard in the aftermath. A starving Europe had to be fed and government war debts to be paid. January to March 1947 had brought long hard frost and deep, deep snow which had destroyed a huge amount of stored potatoes, resulting in potatoes and bread, not rationed in the war, now rationed. It was the hardest winter in living memory. Morale was quite low because people had experienced years of suffering and expected things to start getting back to normal, not get worse.

A particularly uplifting newsworthy item, that affected the whole country, and was the first of its kind in the world - indeed the envy of the whole world - was the introduction of the National Health Service, 5th July 1948. The day after it had been broadcast on the radio by the Prime Minister, Clement Atlee, Roy proudly and eagerly turned up at his friend's encampment, clutching a newspaper. The travellers were very welcoming:

'EE Ruey yous a good un. We listened to it on the wireless but they jukels'.

Gabriel read Roy's face.

'Dogs......started barking an some of what we did ear didn't mek a lot of sense. What's 'tripartite' mean? 'Roy wasn't sure either.

'Theys just talk fancy to sound clever n' fool us.'

Roy grinned, he agreed but thought it was a case of the

pot calling the kettle black. He couldn't understand the travellers sometimes and marvelled at how, when they spoke amongst themselves they sounded like they were talking backwards, but they made a polite effort for his benefit.

A crowd of people listened intently as he read and explained what he knew about the new health service. They didn't speak until he had stopped:

'EE. Fancy. Well would ee ever 'v believed it? Go on, go on.'

'It won't include us , will it? We look after our own, we don't ask nobody fer nothing. It'll be fer gadges who pay that there national insurance.'

'Yes, Roy assured them, you *are* included – it's for EVERYBODY. Even children and people who don't work and people who come for a holiday from other countries.'

When he'd finished the old woman who seemed to carry the most influence spoke:

'Doctus see EVERYBODY...... FREE, what thinks yous about that then Gabriel?'

The old leprechaun-faced man in the trilby replied

pensively:

'Oi reckon oi'd look kushti in some ov they posh spectacles.'

'What be yous needin spectacles fer? Yous can't read 'n yous don't do the sewin.'

He gave a big toothless grin.

'What yous need Gabriel is some o they posh bright teeth.'

She continued wisely:

'They'll be a lot o folk quein up fer they – big queues.'

Everyone nodded. 'They'll be comin from all overs the world!'

Everyone nodded again, slowly, seriously; then, their faces broke into laughter as Gabriel faced the crowd with a slice of raw potato in his mouth, his lips parted pretending he had white dentures, his forefingers and thumbs circling his eyes like spectacles. He started to dance a jig. Someone put some gramophone music on and everyone eagerly joined in the dancing.

After a great night round the warm fire, jigging and a sort of country dancing and a few tots of whisky in his cordial and some wonga in his pocket, Roy felt blissfully happy and very grown up but he had to go home. He thanked his friends for a 'kushti' evening and set off into the dark night.

He had got so carried away enjoying himself that he had lost track of the time. Away from the fire, alone, it was very dark and cold. He started to shiver with fear as well as cold. The long lane back to his home was unlit. He suddenly realized that he was only a young boy.....with money in his pockets....and very vulnerable! Anyone or anything could pounce out of the shadowy blackness. How he wished he had his dog with him. He had a brainwave. Like most of his friends, who aspired to be grown up, he had a few cigarettes and a box of matches in his pockets. He lit a cigarette and held it high above his head. He stamped his feet hard as he walked. In the dark, he thought, people... or things, would think he was a big, tall man....*not* to be messed with!

Chapter 12.

HIGH EXPECTATIONS.

After the severe winter of 1947 came a really hot summer. Roy and his friends roamed the countryside on their bikes looking for good places to bathe. Polio, a horrible disease that could kill or leave its victim permanently paralyzed, was rife in that year and could be caught from infected water, but these thoughts or any thoughts of health and safety were far from the minds of the friends as they frolicked around in the water of ponds, rivers and canals, enjoying their unfettered freedom and boyhood rivalries. Roy loved to show his daring by diving from bridges. First he would swim in the canal and test the depth of the water. None of the canal water was very deep, but he liked a challenge. The nearest bridge to his home - Grange road bridge, was unsuitable because it had far too many bricks in the canal, but as he got older, he ventured further afield and had a whale of a time diving off most of the bridges between Bedworth and

154

Coventry.

One particularly simmering day, the friends raced on their bikes and practised up and down hills. They were really keen to enter the local cycle speedway rally. These competitions were springing up all over the country. The tracks were made from the rubble of bombed sites. There were hundreds of them in blitzed out London and the craze quickly spread to the rest of the country. Coventry, a world leader in bike manufacturing, had gone cycle crazy. The courses were treacherous, but that was part of the appeal to the young braves; they were well up to the challenge, but sadly their bikes weren't. Still, they competed amongst themselves, undeterred, biking up hills, jumping obstacles and whizzing down slag heaps in their boys' paradise.

After fierce cycling they needed a swim. A favourite place was Hawkesbury Junction - just a field away from Blackhorse Road. The locals called the place Sutton Stop as the first lock keepers there had the surname Sutton. Two canals; the Coventry canal and the Oxford canal, ran side by side there, then converged into one. By the side of the Coventry canal was an old Victorian engine house that once housed the pump that pumped water from nearby mines, and a wooden bridge with great bannisters for sliding down. There was a small iron bridge over the Oxford canal and a narrow part of canal where the lock was, ideal for adventurous boys or drunken men to attempt to jump. On the towpath to the side of this bridge was a beautiful 'olde' pub, 'The Greyhound,' with benches out the front where customers enjoyed the scenery and goings on. A few cottages and many coloured working canal narrow-boats, brightly decorated with canal roses and castles, clustered alongside the pub. A magnificent, elegant Victorian wrought iron bridge, spanning the area between the two smaller bridges, completed the picture or 'playground' for it was a regular jaunt of the boisterous group.

After a dive to be proud of from the wooden bridge, and, feeling a bit cocky, Roy was a bit put out when one of his crowd shouted over:

'Bet you couldn't dive off that one!' He pointed to the high wrought iron bridge.

'Huh, bet I could.'

'Go on then, let's see ya, bet ya daredn't,' sneered the jealous colleague. Roy's mates all looked at him.

'I could do it,' replied Roy 'but I'd want paying, you could crack your skull open divin off that one. You gonna pay me?' knowing full well the lad couldn't pay him.

A few days later Roy's biker mates turned up for him really excited:

'Come on Ruey, you're going to make some money.'

He biked with them, non the wiser; down a path at the side of a field, then up a slight muddy slope which brought them out to Sutton Stop. The boys lifted their bikes and clambered over the wooden bridge. A large crowd had gathered on both sides of the large wrought iron bridge; everyone had come out of the pub, glasses in hand supping up, mostly local miners, and people from off the boats. They applauded as the boys approached.

Roy's friend explained proudly:

'We're making a collection for you to dive off the bridge.' He saw Roy's face. 'You *can* do it can't you. You've dived from that high before.'

Well Roy had, but he'd come very close to cracking his skull and had privately vowed that he wouldn't be that stupid again.

He gulped, sweat trickled from his brow. He felt more unnerved with the large crowd all looking at him – all waiting for him to do it. It was one thing his friends watching, but all these! He gripped the handle bars of his bike. He could whizz off... He knew it wasn't really an option for him though. He was bred to face injury and even death rather than lose face and contemplate cowardice. You just…. got on with it!

He pushed down his bike, to more cheers and walked heavily up the steep slope of the bridge. He usually liked the sound of his footsteps on the wooden planks but today it sounded like a funeral march. In the centre of the bridge he gripped one side of the hard, cold, iron rail and looked down into the shallow, grey water. It seemed further than he'd ever noticed. And all the faces were staring up at him. His hands quivered. How was he even going to get on the rail, his legs had jellified.

His elder brother, Les was surprised to see the sight before him as he came running round the tow path. He was on a five mile jog as part of his boxing training. The crowd all cheered again to see the boxing champ. He looked at Roy, then the canal and horrified, realized what his kid brother was going to attempt. People moved out of the way as Les sprinted up to the top of the bridge.

'Come on, Roy. You're not doing this. You'll crack your head open and kill yourself.'

'They're all waiting. I've got to do it. Anyway, I can't let the family reputation down. You could get killed every time you go in the ring.'

It was true, Les was now fighting world class boxers.

It was a hard act for his young brother to follow. All thoughts of carting Roy away died. He knew there was no stopping him, Roy *had* to do it.

'I don't know why my legs are shaking so much. I've dived this high before.'

'It's like stage fright, Roy. You've got to block out the crowd; they're not there... and focus. Fear's good - channel it; it makes you stronger, more capable. You're gonna do the best dive you've ever done!'

'Do you ever get this frit?

'All the time. All the time. Now focus – a really shallow dive, you know you can do it. Breathe in, and now out slowly, slowly and again.

Les's heart was in his mouth, he felt sick, he hoped his words had convinced Roy more than he believed them himself.

Three deep breaths then Roy climbed up onto the iron hand rail. The crowd held their breath. Roy stared at a spot a long way down... In a flash, he soared through the air: Like a king fisher swooping to catch its prey, he skimmed the murky, shallow water.

The onlookers breathed again as… he surfaced. Dripping wet, he was hauled out by a relieved cheering crowd. None so pleased as his friends who ran round again with their caps of coins.

'You *did* it Roy. We can get the bikes fixed up now and go in the Cycle Speedway Rally.'

The friends had big plans for the money. But Roy wasn't listening; he looked for his brother, but, seeing that Roy was safe, Les had sprinted away, to let Roy enjoy his full glory. Besides, training had to take priority; he'd heard his next opponent was deadly!

Chapter 13.

CYCLE FEVER!

The gang competed amongst themselves to see who was to be in the cycle team, four to a team. They optimistically called themselves 'The Black Horse Champs,' despite being younger than most of the other contestants. They couldn't afford the top of the range bikes, but were able to buy stronger spokes and customise their own bikes.

What had started out with youths racing their bikes around city bomb sites had escalated. It was inspirational to see how much joy and entertainment had come forth from such devastation and horror. The first cycle tracks had been made, with a lot of work by the 'Skid Kids', as the press called them. The bricks and rubble of bombed buildings were used to construct the perimeters of oval shaped tracks of approximately 90 metres. The actual track was just a dirt track. As the sport progressed, rules were agreed and rallies organised, and proper leagues. Villages played one another, then the winner's competed for their area. It ended up with international events and monthly magazines dedicated to it. Organizers were mostly parents of competitors who averaged 13 to 18 years.

Small as it was, even Longford had a team to enter - 'The Longford Dominoes.' Shirley Thompson excitedly went to support her team. Her street, Lady Lane, had even laid on transport. She climbed on the back of Marlowe's open topped coal lorry, which they'd all spent time cleaning for the occasion and sat on a comfy bale of hay.

Now ten years old, she'd earned some money for the day out by washing the floors in the back storage rooms of a local shop. On her hands and knees she'd washed up vinegar from the vats mixed with cat wee on the floor. Sometimes they let her serve in the shop which had very little in it to sell and every time they had a customer she had to tap on the back window and ask the old lady 'Have we got any......?' The old woman would look at the customer through the window and nod or shake her head. If 'yes,' Shirley would serve the customer from the goods under the counter, weighing and wrapping things with care.

Today, Sunday, most shops were closed and most people off work. Working hours, especially for men were typically very long but Sunday was a day of rest and enjoyment.

The Marlowe family took Shirley with them on most of their outings, luckily, because her own mother had painful bunion feet and was distressed if she ventured out of the street. Alice seemed content though to spend the Sunday afternoon with the radio on and her Dickens and Dick Barton novels.

The cycle speedway rally was a well organized event. Shirley had the largest ice- cream cornet that the ice cream van sold. Then she bought a raffle ticket and got a good seat, on a bend, for the exciting event. Hundreds of people had turned up to watch.

The starting and finishing line looked like a football goalpost. A recent improvement was the starting method, now using a white line, of the sort of elastic put in knickers, pulled tightly across. It gave a fairer start than shouting 'go' as no one could set off too early. A man in a long white coat (like a cricket umpire or painter and decorator) pulled the elastic from the inside giving the outsiders a very slight starting advantage. All very official. The competitors set off from a standstill - 4 boys at a time, with 3 points for the winner 2 for second and 1 for third. It went on for 14 races of 4 times round the track.

The precise care given to the start of the race, and positions didn't make a terrible lot of difference once the race began. It was a mad, dangerous free for all. The bikes had no gears or breaks. The competitors used their inside foot on the ground to balance and slow down round bends. The frightening, fearless speed that they went, wrecked their shoes and their bike tyres. Competitors needed nerves and wrists of steel. Despite all this there was no lack of youngsters eager to participate.

Roy's big moment had come. He stared at the starting tape, a serious gladiator stare. Whoosh, they were off. He was very fit and not lacking in bravery. He had practised on hills. The crowd all shouted loudly for their teams. He was one in from the outside. He gave it all he'd got to try and get past the others so that he could get on the inside ring. The next bike in had got the latest speedway handlebars. They were like big cow horns, designed to help balance, but the rider, like most, used them to keep pushing Roy's bike away, interrupting his rhythm. On the third lap he managed to get ahead enough to cross over into the inside. Pedalling like crazy he was just ahead of the others when suddenly he'd got to the bend. This he hadn't practiced much. He leaned over with his foot down on the floor, making a groove in the track, but he was taking it too fast - the bike went over. The one behind crashed into him. The young gladiator was abruptly on all fours in a cloud of dust with a bike pedal up his backside. The crowd were standing up eager not to miss the entertainment. Trembling, he climbed back on his bike and tried to finish the race, but his bike wasn't up to it; his nose and his knee dripped with blood mixed with dust - his pride hurt more!

He hadn't been a total failure though. Shirley had marvelled at how brave he was. For her he was the hero of the day.

He held his nose for a few minutes, to stop his nose bleed, then pumped up his bike wheel and got a good front spot to clap the winners. First, they called the raffle. Shirley had won first prize. Flicking her long, auburn plaits back, she climbed on stage. The prize made her eyes sparkle; it was a massive basket of fruit and jars of food, biscuits and chocolates; luxuries she rarely tasted. She wondered if Mrs Marlowe who'd organized the raffle had played a part in her winning. Wouldn't her mum be pleased! Shirley's tiny face lit up; she smiled her widest, exuberant smile.

'Wow ! ... Roy had never seen such a smile; what a beauty. Standing there, all dusty in his ripped trousers with red nostrils, Roy gave her his coolest wink. She blushed - as red as her hair.

***

That evening at home, Shirley was not with the rest of the family - she was in her own little dream world. She kept smiling to herself in a real daze.

167

'Winning that raffle's gone to her head,' her sister's decided. But the raffle wasn't what Shirley was thinking about; at the fledgling age of ten, she'd made up her mind who she wanted to marry.

Chapter 14.

ODD JOBS AND PEOPLE!

'Ruey!' a voice called from somewhere behind Roy, 'Just the person I need to talk to.'

Roy, now thirteen, was just peacefully walking his dog along the canal towpath. He turned to face the woman climbing up the steps of the cabin of her narrow -boat.

'I wants to ask you a big favour. We's got a big problem, wiv going up 'n' down the cut all the time I never gots any decent schoolin. Our Thomas wants is educashun - its important, very important! But the problem is ' e can't get to school without bein beat up.'

Roy thought that they, like his gypsy friends who went away fruit picking in the summer, were really lucky not to have to do much schooling. He had never really liked it. He thought back to when he started school. After his first few days, he had decided that he wasn't going any more, and ran off at school time. Maud was in despair. A neighbour offered to help. The next morning, he turned up at the house, caught Roy, tied his hands to his shoes and put him in the back of his car, only untying him in the school playground.

Roy sympathised with the boat people about the bullying though. His elder brother 'Les' had experienced the same thing as a child. His only crime for the merciless bullying was wearing glasses.

Roy had heard bully's taunting the boat people:

'Boaty, boaty piss in the cut. Dirty Boaty.'

It was true that the boat people had a hard job keeping clean with their cargoes of coal and the coal dust got *everywhere*. They were worn out at the end of the journeys, after all the canal locks, long hours to achieve their targets and watching that the horses that pulled the boats didn't get their rope tangled and fall in; then fetching their own water and supplies.

Les, Roy and the middle brother Don had all been enrolled on boxing lessons and were now a match for anyone. Les, eight years older than Roy, had really excelled at the sport and was becoming a local boxing celebrity.

The woman continued:

'We wondered if you'd do us a big favour 'n' let our Thomas walk to school wiv you Ruey. He'll be safe then!'

Roy was glad to help; the boat people at Sutton Stop had always made time to chat to him, since he was able to talk.

'No problem, I'll look after him. Tell him its number 200 Blackhorse Road. He can call for me on Monday. I'll make sure nobody touches him, Mrs Smith, don't you worry!'

'You're a good un Ruey. We's got a sugar cargo on the other boat I'll make sure your mam has some.'

Well, Roy was full of good intentions, but before school, whilst it was still dark, he went lamping with his dog to get rabbits for dinner; a regular venture. He shone a strong beam of light on the rabbits and they froze, allowing the dog to run and pick them up. The dark mornings of autumn had crept up and Roy didn't realise the time. He wasn't normally that bothered about being late for school, even though he got the cane. After putting his burning hands on a cold radiator, he enjoyed the hero status amongst his classmates. Besides, his teacher seemed to cane him even when he tried his best. At first the painful, cruel punishment had been traumatic but gradually he had become accustomed to it. He couldn't see the blackboard very clearly after measles had left him almost blind in one eye, but there was no way he was going to follow his brother with thick glasses so bluffed his way along and acted naughty if asked to read from the blackboard.. But, he hadn't meant for poor Thomas to suffer. After avoiding the bullying children and managing to get to school, Thomas got wacked for not being on time, mercilessly, by the teacher - with the same half- inch thick rod that was now used on Roy.

The only reparation that Roy managed was to threaten the other children not to ever touch Thomas so that he was able to continue his 'education' on time.

Roy was becoming a strong young man. He loved sparring with his brothers but wasn't really interested in boxing in the ring; however they insisted on taking him with them to matches and when someone didn't turn up his brothers would push him in the boxing ring. On his eighteenth birthday, Les left his mining job at the pit for good to box professionally. Roy was just ten, but he went with Les all over the country to boxing matches, watching over Les; in London he even tasted Les's food and drink to make sure that it wasn't drugged by some of the unsavoury characters they encountered. His brother always wanted him with him, and Roy always wanted to go. When Les's manager, who owned a butchers shop, brought massive steaks to build his star up for the fights, Les made sure his younger sibling had one.

Back home his brother Don was working delivering coal with a lorry. Roy would join Don and they would get paid extra by people for carrying the sacks of coal round the back gardens and shovelling it into the coal bunkers. This paid more than their childhood ventures which had included chopping up bundles of wood and selling them and starting a fruit and veg stall in their Andersen shelter.

But despite all this he was reminded that he was still, officially, a child. His mother, normally lenient wouldn't let him go with Les when he started going to fight abroad, starting with Milan in 1950. She thought it too dangerous and he needed to finish his schooling. She was right about the dangers. Fights were not often filmed and to win in Italy, Les said that you had to knock your opponent out. The refs wouldn't dare let you win on points. In Rome he was tripped up on the way to the ring and the angry mob threw shoes and rotten food at him in the boxing arena.

Back at school his elder brother's success had made it difficult for Roy at first. Older boys had challenged him to fights so that they could brag that they had beaten Les Allen's brother, but he had trained with the best and learned well and soon proved himself a match for the bullies. Now, with only a year to go to school, he was enjoying school football and peer group popularity, but his teacher seemed to hate him. He sadistically caned Roy with the extra thick cane at every opportunity. At the end of a particularly boring school day Roy was just putting his chair on his desk along with the rest of the class, to leave a clear floor for the cleaners, when: 'CRACK' – the full force of the cane came down, smashed between his shoulder blades. Instinctively, he swung round, cracking the wooden chair against the teacher's head. Seeing the bloodied teacher lying on the floor, Roy panicked and ran, escaping through the classroom window and sprinting to the safety of home.

The teacher recovered but Roy was suspended from school, whilst it was decided what to do with him. It was thought that he would be sent away to an approved school, a Borstal. He was really worried He'd heard it was like a prison. He was naturally quiet; loving his home, his family, his many pets, and he'd been looking forward to getting a decent job when he left school. It didn't improve the contempt his family held for authority.

Les gave him a job to do to occupy him. With the money he'd already made from boxing Les wanted to buy the old cottage, 'Frog's Hall' that he'd lived in and loved as a child. Now that he had a car, living in the middle of a field would no longer be the hardship that it had been. But though, still picturesque, the cottage had dilapidated. It wouldn't be too difficult to renovate, but no- one would be allowed to live in it unless it had drinkable water approved by the local water authority and, unfortunately, the well - the only source of drinking water, was all clogged up.

Les gave Roy some money to hire some mates and get it sorted. There was no shortage of offers of help and Roy chose three brothers, a bit younger than him and known to be a bit rough; he chose them because they looked really keen and like they needed the money more than most. All alike, from a large family; they had the large hungry-eyed, frightened look of poverty.

He had judged correctly. They certainly were eager to help. When they got to the cottage they excitedly all wanted to be the one to go down the well on the rope. How would he choose? They were all looking at him with those desperate eyes that filled their thin faces. He tossed a coin, the winner of the first toss went into the second round. The middle- sized one won.

He wasn't sure who was who because they all looked so alike. There was said to be 17 of them in the family which may have been an exaggeration but they seemed to always be everywhere so perhaps it was true.

'Don't worry. You'll all get a go,' he promised.

They helped the first one onto the rope, with his legs crossed, like he was sitting on the well bucket. He was instructed to feel around and bring some rubbish up in the bucket when they wound him back up. The rope, like the house had seen better days and they heard a loud splash as the rope snapped. Roy ran over to the house; he had seen a ladder propped up there. He ran back to the well and started to lower it down. Terror gripped him as he was left holding a few rungs of rotten ladder. He shouted down. No answer! He couldn't see anyone. He ran back to the house, desperately looking for another ladder, another rope – anything! He could find nothing! He ran back to the well. The older brother was putting a metal cover over the well.

'He must be dead! Come on… RUN!'

Roy couldn't believe his ears – this was his own brother, he was about to leave; he was clearly morally impoverished as well as financially. Roy pulled the cover off and threw it to the ground.

Immense relief poured over them all as they heard:

'Cough, cough, cough, cough, cough f****** get me out quick you f****** w******!'

Somehow he'd managed to clamber onto the bit of ladder; there he stayed while Roy ran to the nearest home, a caravan that one of his own uncles lived in with his wife and 5 children. There he got the help that they needed.

It didn't deter the nearly drowned boy and his fugitive brothers. With better equipment they did a good job on the well and a few days later the helpers of all ages celebrated with fresh clean water and a drop of moonshine whisky.

The water board Inspector was sent for and took a sample away with him.

Disappointedly a letter arrived saying that the water was *'... not of a suitable standard.'* Maud was indignant:

'We drank from that well for years – the water's as healthy as any. What's his game?'

As ever she was not giving in without a fight. She visited the water-board official's office a week later.

'The well's been cleaned more thoroughly, if you'd be kind enough to test the water again? I've brought a sample of the water here to save you having to go all the way out there again......And some front row tickets for Les's next fight.'

The official's eyes gleamed at the tickets.

'Yes I'd be glad to Mrs Allen, but I can't promise anything. I have to do my job.'

He thought it wouldn't hurt to humour the silly old fool. For a proper inspection he'd have to go out but he knew the outcome already.

Maud knew all about some officials 'doing their job.'

Estate agents and their official friends often bought properties themselves at a much reduced price because the properties were said to have not passed official tests. Still she pandered to him sweetly.

The letter arrived; not surprisingly the water still hadn't passed the standard and was deemed '*unfit for drinking.*'

Maud put on her best hat and gloves and paid another visit to the Inspector.

'I'm sorry to hear that the water's not fit to drink Inspector, because I made a mistake and brought the wrong water. That was out of our tap at home – the drinking water that you supply to the whole area………….. We know some good press men through my son's boxing - who might be very interested.'

The inspector's sunny smile turned stormy. Silently he filled in the form of approval and pushed it over to her.

Why was the damned woman still sitting with her hand outstretched?

'Tickets, please!' she commanded: 'We're a bit choosy about who sits in the front row.'

**

Maud needed the front row tickets – she had another official to face.

The Education official came to her home. Fingers crossed that he liked boxing. It was extremely popular. Every week, before television became widespread, people could have a night out watching a local boxing match, but to see boxing of the championship standard that her son displayed was a rare treat. Mostly men went to the matches and women listened on the radio, but some women went with their partners. Major stars such as Diana Dors went to see fights featuring Maud's son from the small council estate. Famous people such as the comedian 'Tommy Trinder' stayed at their council house full of people and dogs.

Boxing clubs were everywhere, schools, even in church halls.....but would the education official be interested, or like the teacher that had caused the problem, be inflamed by it all – her son's future depended on it!

The family didn't know whether the official was influenced just by the whisky and boxing tickets, or genuinely by Maud's rendition of the teacher's long term abuse towards her son and how the deed was accidental; but, whatever his reason, he decided to let Roy return to the school on condition that he apologise to the teacher. This took even more powers of Maud's persuasiveness. Roy always spoke his mind truthfully, whatever the consequences and found it the most difficult thing he ever had to do.

He went back to school for his final year with a fresh teacher wondering what to expect. The new teacher likewise, was very apprehensive. He had a private talk with Roy:

'I want no trouble Roy. If you want to come in and get your mark and go and work on the school allotment or even go home. You'll have no trouble from me. I'm here to teach and I want pupils who want to learn. This last year's a very important educational year.'

Roy had never had a teacher who spoke to him frankly and like an adult. He learnt more in that last year than most of his school life. He could ask for help without being ridiculed and responded by being punctual and attentive. He was amazed when he came second in the class at mathematics. He was also able to put the other talents that he had learnt at school to good use: The teacher got to know him and found out that he never picked on anyone and asked Roy as a personal favour if he would use his fighting skills to stamp out the bullying that was rife in the school. How could he refuse – he just wasn't destined for a quiet life.

Chapter 15.

EARNING A CRUST.

Fifteen years old, at last. Roy was jubilant. He'd never got to do another day at school. He could earn more money. But, what was he to do? His brothers had both started off at local pits, following their dad. They had managed to move onto better things. His dad, however had stayed there long enough to suffer chronic chest complaints, as did most long term miners. Roy remembered standing with women and children, not knowing if their loved ones would return from a nearby pit that flooded a lot and had, before he was born, trapped hundreds and suffocated 14 miners in one tragic incident. Not knowing if their loved ones would return from the black hole, their anguished faces were etched on his memory. He shuddered at the thought of it; he liked to be out in the open air. He joined his mother in the kitchen for a cup of tea. The kitchen was used more as a consulting surgery than for cooking. Just about everyone from Blackhorse road came to Maud for advice and home-made lotions. Whatever problem Roy had, she was always there and he never had to tell her he had a problem. She knew by looking at him; and, thanks to her highly developed intelligence network or her uncanny intuitiveness, she usually knew what the problem was. This was lucky for him, because he wasn't a winger and would have just bottled up his problems inside, silently. Today was no exception; she sat down at the table and poured them both a cup of tea:

'Our Roy, I've been talking to Jack Gilbert and they're willing to take you on as an apprentice at the bakery in Bedworth.' His mum was just amazing:

'A bakery. Gilberts bakery. But I can't cook – Jack Gilberts bakery?' he really hadn't thought of anything like this.

Jack Gilbert had married his elder sister, Sheila and had come to live in their front room until they got their own house. Jack's family were considered highly respectable and well to do, not least of all by themselves. Many shopkeepers were like this. The war rationing had bequeathed them almost god-like status as they could decide who had some items of under the

185

counter food. Roy was surprised Jack had agreed to it. Roy and his brothers had mimicked him, mercilessly behind his back. He must have seen some of it. They just couldn't help it. He was so particular and prim and proper. He clearly thought he had married below him and certainly wouldn't mix with their friends. He had plans to remove Sheila from this rabble. Everything had to be just so for him. Even his drink. He kept his lemonade in a bottle in a tub of cold water in the pantry in the day and then put it by his bedside at night. On hot days they all looked at it wistfully but knew that it was strictly out of bounds. As was his beautiful, gleaming new motorbike that he kept at the side of the house. He wasn't known for sharing with people he didn't trust. Well for all his perceived airs and graces, he had a good side. Maud continued diplomatically:

'You'd be perfect for the job, Roy. You love to get up early and you're so good with horses. You'd be taking the horse out on the round and they'd teach you to bake the bread and cakes. We'd never want for cakes.'

Put in that context Roy thought it sounded marvellous.

186

Especially the thought of being up on the bread- round cart in charge of a magnificent shire horse; then cakes for all his friends. Gilbert's cakes were very sought after.

Some young men would have found being in charge of a big delivery cart and colossus horse a bit daunting, but although he had never owned one himself, Roy had quite a bit of experience with horses, albeit sometimes painful. Only the week before he had had a great time: A traveller friend's herd of horses had got out of their enclosure and he had helped round them up, riding bareback. His eyes beamed.

He went to work bright and early with Jack on his first day at 5 in the morning. This wasn't too early for him. Everyone outside his family called him 'Ruey'. It had started off as 'Rooster' because he got up with the first cock crow at dawn, then shortened to 'Ruey'.

It was explained to him that he wouldn't be able to take the horses out until he had learnt enough and they felt that they could trust him. They had taken him on a bit reluctantly, with a lot of persuasion from his pretty sister because they had thought he was a bit too young and a bit wild. He was undeterred though; he'd just have to learn it all and show them. He proved to be a quick learner and worked very hard. The Gilbert family were really pleased. He was given more and more responsibility. His job wasn't learning to prepare the bread and cakes, but when someone was off he volunteered to go at night to help prepare them for the next day. He enjoyed putting two fingers in the top of the dough on the cottage loaves then marking them with a razor.

Early next morning he would help get the hot bread trays out of the oven, breathing in the wonderful smell; and whilst the fresh bread was cooling he would get on with his favourite job of getting the horses ready.

He tended them lovingly, rubbing them down, making their coats gleam, polishing the harnesses; giving them a bag of oats and fresh water. He would blow in their ears and they would snuffle in his pockets. He didn't even mind cleaning the carts and mucking out. He couldn't wait for the day he'd be allowed to take one out himself.

The day finally arrived. It was a lot sooner than they had said. Still only fifteen, he had earnt enough respect from his employers to be entrusted to take a large horse and cart out on his own, delivering daily bread and cakes piled up high and collecting the money. He hoped they wouldn't give him 'Major.'

Major was named after Jack's dad, the owner of the bakery. It was said that Mr Gilbert had been a sergeant major in the armed forces and had saved up all his money to buy the bakery; he certainly ran it with the efficiency of a sergeant major. Standards were very high, the horse mucking out and grooming and the quality of the daily baked bread and cakes. The horse 'Major' had been a point to point race horse in his time and apart from his tendency to nip you if you upset him, he'd once bolted and smashed his cart into a shoe shop window. Roy's employer's sensibly gave him 'Tommy,' a gentler big brown horse that was half cart-horse. His route wasn't so easy though. Gilbert's bakery supplied the whole of Bedworth and Tommy's route included a steep hill.

They set off, the young man, proud as punch and his regal equine workmate, delivering their ware from a large green cart; starting on the main Black Bank road by the bakery and making their way round Bedworth ending up on the outskirts. The horse knew every stop. It went like a dream, until with just one street to go, they ran out of bread. They had to go all the way back to the bakery for more and the horse wouldn't hurry. Still, Mrs Gilbert was well pleased with how much they'd sold.

The next day, feeling confident and perhaps a bit cocky, Roy thought he'd try a better way. If he started the round at the furthest point, which was now the end and worked his way back, it would be much nearer the bakery to fetch extra should he run out and be much quicker. Tommy plodded very slowly, however much Roy urged him, he didn't seem to have a higher gear. But Roy thought it would still be a lot quicker this way.

He got down from his cart and loaded the orders for the next few houses in his basket. He knocked on the first door.

'Hello, is it the usual today? Is there anything else I can tempt you with – some hot jam doughnuts perhaps?' He sounded like he'd been doing it for years.

'You're early today,' the customer smiled.

'Yes I thought it would be quicker to start this end first,' he explained.

'Not without a horse, it won't.' she replied, looking down the street.

He followed her gaze and saw Tommy running – *yes* he could run - *fast*! He was having none of it. Cart horses don't like change. They are as unchanging as oak trees and Tommy knew his familiar route. Roy chased him frantically all the way back, over 5 miles, as he went in a roundabout way, right back to his first stop.

From then on Roy carried on conventionally; he had found out who was in charge – Tommy. The winter was icy cold; Tommy had to have frost studs put on his hooves to help stop him slipping but he still came down the steep hill on his backside. And Roy encountered a really worrying problem. His mother

191

knew there was something up, but what? He assured her his employers were treating him well. He gave her his board as usual. She didn't take much from him now that most of them were working and Les was doing really well. Just enough to get him in good habits but she couldn't understand why he wasn't going out spending his money. None of his friends could persuade him to go out. Perhaps he was saving for a car or something. Even his boots looked worn. He wouldn't be scruffy by choice. And he looked so miserable.

She knew it was no good just asking him, he never told her any of his problems. She decided to visit an old friend who conveniently lived on Roy's bread round.

'You know it's our Roy who delivers the bread now, don't you Hilda?'

'Your Roy, little Ruey, grown up that quick. Where does the time go? Oh he's a saint. They're calling him the Robin Ood of Beduth, you must be very proud of him. Little Rooey. Who'd ave thought it, little Ruey.'

'They're calling him *what?...Why?*'

'Well, he never lets nobody go short of bread, even if they ain't got no money.'

**

'Had a good day Robin?' she greeted him when he came home from work.

'I didn't mean it to happen Mam. It just happened. It was a poor family, they had kids and they looked hungry. When I got back, I got into trouble. They said don't let anybody have anything unless they can pay. But they looked so hungry, so I put my own money in. But then more and more of them needed bread. They say they'll pay me when they can. But there seems to be more of them every week. I can't do it. I can't say no to people needing bread.'

'No, I expect I'd be the same, but that's not the job for you. I'll have a word with Jack. You'll have to leave.'

The relief oozed from his young face. He had tried so hard.

'Well, you'll never be rich, that's for sure, but I'm proud of you.' She kissed his forehead, now free of lines.

'Please don't tell the others. I'll be a laughing stock.' he pleaded. They both laughed.

But it wasn't funny for Jack. The others didn't know why Roy had left. They'd just seen him unhappy and were fiercely loyal. Maud had just settled down to bed when, she heard Jack shouting in the hallway.

'Come on, who's done it? It's one of you! It's got to be one of you! Maud, I just can't take any more of this I'm from a respectable family I am, respectable. They're heathens! Heathens!'

'Now calm down Jack and tell me what's the matter.'

Everyone was up now and watching from the stairs.

He was so upset he could hardly get the words out:

' I swigged my pop down'.

'Yes, go on' Maud coaxed.

'But it's not my pop.........they've poisoned me. **I've been poisoned!** Someone's....... **piddled** in me pop!!!'

Everyone on the stairs hooted with laughter. Maud had to put her hand over her mouth to hide her own laughter.

She was a born diplomat though; she eventually managed to calm Jack and everyone down and maintain the status quo…but not for long. A quiet life just wasn't possible in that house, in that neighbourhood. The Blackhorse road community wasn't quite a smuggler's den like you read about in Cornish history but it was very close knit and a bit contemptuous of the law – survival was priority.

One day a friend came running in the kitchen, hot and breathless:

'The coppers ' r' coming – you better be quick!'

Previously he had brought the family a present – some chickens.

They had plucked them and two were cooking in the oven, five more lay on the kitchen table.

One of the brother's had an idea.

'Sheila, give us the keys to your room, quick!'

Sheila handed them over. Since the pop incident Jack had locked the room he shared with Sheila. He was just having his afternoon nap.

The police came to search the house. The policemen

were not the local ones and not known to the family - so not open to Maud's persuasion. They didn't even listen when she told them that it was 'Jack Gilbert' that was asleep in the front room - from the *respectable* 'Gilbert' family. They just woke him from his snoring dreams to find himself surrounded by dead, plucked chickens, looking up at policemen; then carted off to the police station!

Luckily at the police station his family's good name got him reprieved, but his embarrassment was too much. He went to see his mother and related his sorry tale while his charming wife listened:

' ...And that's not all of it! Mother, you just wouldn't believe what goes on in that house. They're crazy.'

His mother had some sympathy:

'Yes I remember someone telling me years ago, that when someone came to the front door they ran and put a baby in the bathroom. We never did find out what that was all about.'

It was true, Joyce had returned from Scotland after an unhappy, short marriage and they had decided that

Maud and Capel would adopt baby Albert even though they'd already had five children of their own. Joyce would then be free again to attract a decent husband. She was very lucky that she had such caring parents because many single women had to part with their baby's often never seeing them again. It took a bit of sorting though and luckily baby Albert was quite happy to be bundled into the downstairs bathroom sucking a sweetened dummy.

'We have to get Sheila away from that lot, mother,' Jack pleaded.

Sheila smiled sweetly – very glad, that little Julie, (who Maud and Capel also adopted), looked more like her American G.I. Father, than herself!

Chapter 16.

BEDWORTH'S GOLDEN BOY.

There was never a dull day at the Allen household; the children made sure of that. The 30th May 1954 was more exciting than usual; it was like the night before xmas for children and for the parents (anxious that all should go well the next day). The whole of Blackhorse road felt it, and most of Bedworth and much of Coventry. But especially at 200 Blackhorse Road, where the cause of all this excitement came from - 'Les Allen junior.' He was now 24 years old and had given up his job at the local pit to box professionally. He was accustomed to professional fights. He had just won his last 12 consecutive, professional fights. He was the Midlands Middleweight Champion, fighting top fighters in a golden age of boxing. He had travelled all over the UK boxing, including Liverpool, Manchester, Nottingham, Newcastle, Cardiff and London then overseas to: Belfast, Northern Ireland; Gothenburg, Sweden; Milan, Italy and Johannesburg,

South Africa. His brother, Roy, now 16 always accompanied him in the UK, but their mother wouldn't allow him to go abroad; she considered it too dangerous. She wasn't wrong; it was a violent sport both in and out of the ring. In London they had met gangsters and Roy's mother never knew that he had to keep a careful eye on Les's food and drink, sometimes even sampling it to make sure that no-one was drugging his brother. He had guarded the dressing room so that Les could have a rest before the matches.

Overseas Les had faced worse, but had shown fearless courage, both inside and outside the arena; having shoes and smelly fruit thrown at him; being tripped up by angry crowds; fighting with broken ribs. The only thing that had really upset him was the horrifying apartheid that he had witnessed in South Africa. He made many friends amongst the black boxers, giving them the hospitality of his home when they were in the UK. It took exceptional self- discipline, courage and bravery to achieve Les's standard.

Roy was so proud of his brother; Les looked every inch the professional boxer, with enormous, bulging arm muscles and a firm impenetrable torso. His ears were slightly ripped where the laces used to tie the boxing gloves had caught him. Inside, he was kind and golden-hearted.

But tonight, Roy sensed that Les wasn't himself. The two of them went for a quiet walk.

Roy's mind cast back to where it had all started. As a child Les had to wear large, thick-lensed glasses. He couldn't pick a coin up off the floor without them. On the way to school, some of the other boys taunted him and knocked his glasses off. Whilst he was fumbling on all fours trying to pick them up, they kicked him to the floor chanting: 'Four Eyes.'

His parents responded by sending the three elder boys; Les, Don and Roy to boxing lessons at the Kings Head pub in Bedworth. Many pubs had boxing lessons then, as did schools and churches. It was a *huge* national sport. Before championship fights were freely available on television; people went to watch local boxing matches weekly. Men would get up especially early to hear American fights on the radio, before going to work, and many women excitedly joined them.

The three boys sparred and skipped and thoroughly enjoyed the sport. Roy and Don did well, winning Midlands championships. Don had even toyed with professional boxing, but Les *really* excelled. He was a local hero. When he went away for fights, trains were put on just for his supporters with flags and banners. One of his trainers also ran a butcher's shop and brought him massive steaks to eat; Les always included Roy in the feasts. He was Roy's hero.

Les was deep in thought for much of the walk, then he spoke determinedly:

'Roy, tell 'em all not to bet on *me!* He's good! He's *really* good! Don't let them lose their money.'

His opponent, American 'Bobby Dawson', was *formidable*. He had just won his last 12 fights. In the previous fight he had beaten 'Yolande Pompey,' who had never been professionally beaten before, and was normally a higher weight than Bobby which makes a big difference in boxing. Bobby, the American dream, was ranked 4th best middleweight champion… *in the World*!

The local excitement was heightened by the fact that this champion was coming to the little town of Bedworth at the Oval, the local football ground.

Bobby had a really vicious left hook and used a bola punch which thrust upwards with maximum force; Les was likely to get a *very* savage pummelling. But he was more worried about letting everyone down.

His kid brother tried to be reassuring:

'You know what mam says: *'You can only do your best. You **can't** do better. So no point worrying!'*

'I just wish I could see well,' Les continued.

Roy laughed:

'Les that's not a *handicap*, that's an *advantage* – your opponent can't tell by *your* eyes what you're going to do!'

They both laughed.

Worrying didn't slow down time; the big day was quickly upon them!

The official ticket sale was 5000 in Bedworth's small oval, but the local people on the ticket door were letting all their friends in free as well. *Everyone* wanted to be there! It was the most exciting event to have *ever* taken place in Bedworth. Spectators were high up the trees; on the roofs of the changing rooms and sheds......The whole place was *pulsating* with tribal expectation!

Roy had never been so worried. His brother hadn't spoken so negatively about a fight before. Psychologically you have a *lot* more chance of winning if you believe you can. It wasn't good to go into a fight with the handicap of self- doubt. Added to that the pressure of everyone you know being there, depending on you. Inwardly Roy prayed that his brother would survive the arena alive to see another day! The crowd were going wild!

***

Roy had been proud of his brother before. After this

day he was bowled over with pride. Everyone who watched Les **beat** the invincible, remembered that day with awe. It shook the sporting world! The press called him 'Bedworth's Golden Boy.'

That night Bedworth loudly, drunkenly celebrated …..except Les and Roy. They went to the hospital!

Les, who had passed his test sat in the driving seat groaning while Roy, still only 16, changed the gears for him and helped drive. Les thought he had broken ribs. How he drove at all in such excruciating pain was incredible; the same tenacious superhero spirit that kept him boxing through the pain barrier.

The hospital x-rays showed that the ribs weren't broken, but there was internal bleeding and bruising. The punches had thrust up *under* his ribs. He was allowed to go home.

Still with his biggest fan assisting, Les drove back to the house he shared with his lovely wife, Margaret. There was only one double bed. Les slept in the middle, Margaret one side of him….. and Roy the other!

'Aaaaagh don't move,' Les groaned. 'This is *worse* than when I fought with broken ribs.'

'Yeah but you did it Les, you bloody did it, you showed em!'

'Yeah Roy, I did it, didn't I?.....I did it......ha ...I did it!!!' It hurt him to laugh but he grinned from ear to cauliflower ear, a lovely big satisfied grin that remained on his face as, exhausted but happy... he slept.

Chapter 17.

A CLASS OF HER OWN.

Shirley was now the shining star of the little Longford church school. Her teachers were elated and couldn't praise her enough; she had passed her eleven plus exam and was going to be the first girl ever from that school to go to grammar school – a very prestigious grammar school - 'Stoke Park'.

Even her dad was proud of her – not an easy achievement for a girl. She badly craved his approval. He didn't have a lot of time for his girls. He worked long hours, and went to the pub after with his work mates, then attended his allotment, then had a water bailiff job, checking that anglers had fishing licences and when he had time did a bit of angling himself. Shirley saw this last pastime as her chance to spend some time with him – he wasn't so keen:

'It's not for girls; how can the men have a piddle if girls are around?'

She wasn't easy to shake off though and tagged along watching the angling intently and, mostly to get her to be quiet, he showed her what to do and let her have a go occasionally.

When he was at work she sneaked out with his best fishing tackle and practised. Tragedy struck when she got her hook caught on some brambles the other side of the river. Her dad made it all look much easier. Horrified she waded in the river and returned home wet and muddy.

The next secret session was even more tragic; trying to do a perfect cast, she hooked her cat that had followed her. The hook lodged firmly in its stomach. Crying all the way she carried the cat on the bus to the free RSPCA van.

The kind vet sorted it and gave her a note for her mother:

'Please do not send this young child on her own again. It is too distressing for her!'

Still she carried on with her angling attempts with

defiant determination. She had a real need to improve. She had heard her dad telling men, angling with their sons, about the Coventry kids annual angling competition. She put her name down. Wally laughed when she told him:

'There's no point you going in, you'll never win – you talk too much.'

But, he did spend a bit more time teaching her.

Finally the big day arrived. About 300 children entered sitting along the canal from the bridge by Courtaulds factory to Sutton Stop and many more came to watch. Sadly Shirley's dad couldn't be there he had gone away for the weekend on a coach with his friends organised by his local pub. He needed his little holidays.

She wasn't on her own though. Her little band of supporters, village children who had laughed when she waded through the mud and helped when she hooked the cat, were all there to cheer her on and talk to her.

And talk and laugh they all did. She wasn't that

bothered about winning with her dad not there and was just enjoying it - so much that she didn't even notice when her float disappeared; luckily someone shouted out. Then they all got really excited as the float disappeared again and again. Somehow Shirley won the match!

Not only was she clapped and cheered on the day; she went with her dad; (her mother wanted to go but felt ill if she travelled out of their street), to a prize- giving meal with the Lord Mayor and was given a gold and silver medal to keep, a shiny cup with her name on to keep for a year and a handbag with money in. Her photograph was in the local Coventry newspaper. Her dad was indeed proud....of his achievement of teaching his daughter, and celebrated more, up the pub.

Unfortunately he wasn't proud enough of her to buy her a new school uniform, but even the second- hand one cost quite a lot. Some poor children got grants for a new uniform, but her family didn't qualify because her dad earnt too much at the Rolls Royce factory. A cream coloured blouse with red piping and a red and gold tie, a skirt below her knees and ¾ grey socks up to her knees, two pairs of lace-up shoes for indoors and outdoors, a navy gymslip, special pens; the list was endless, but best of all - a smart *new* hat with a red and gold band. She thought it was wonderful as she proudly kept trying it on. She'd never worn anything as smart. She caught the two buses to her new school then walked three miles, then down the long school drive to Stoke Park, girl's grammar school.

She was no longer the shining star of the school as many of the children there had private tuition; she certainly stood out from the crowd though, and no longer felt proud and smart - how she longed for their uniforms to fade!

Their privileges in life didn't make them better people. In the playground one day, a girl was enjoying tormenting everyone with a worm on a stick. She cornered one little girl who was scared of worms. Shirley, took the worm from her and threw it away. Little Mary never forgot. Neither did the bully; she was not one to be beaten! She sat behind Shirley in class and pulled her long plaits hard making some titter quietly. Shirley went red and continued with her handwriting. Having achieved her goal the girl did it again….and again! Then a pin was stuck in Shirley's back. Whoosh, the lid flew off the kettle and Shirley swung round and bashed the girl's hand onto the desk and pummelled it with her fist; the teacher struggled to stop her.

These girls had not experienced open violence and defiance of this kind, neither had the teacher….or the headmistress. When the screaming had stopped, they weren't sure what to do. The other girl had been very sneaky and denied everything. Punishments at this school usually just took the form of an order mark, seven order marks and you had your name read out in assembly in the dishonours list.

It was decided that, largely due to the glowing report of Shirley's primary teachers, she wouldn't be expelled but she would certainly never be teacher's pet at this school.

As the other uniforms faded a little Shirley got used to

her new environment and started to enjoy some of the lessons. She learnt hockey and tennis. She excelled at art and handwriting. She particularly loved drawing historic, Greek and Roman buildings with their Doric and Ionian columns. She wasn't very musical, most of her peers had played an instrument from a young age. She got weekly disciplinary order marks at cookery for forgetting her ingredients; she was too proud to admit that her mum couldn't afford them, but wasn't very bothered about the order mark punishments and her name read out in assembly regularly. She found Latin difficult and she also had to master speaking English correctly, not just for elocution lessons - all the time really to fit in. This was very difficult because at home everyone called her 'miss la de dah' and 'high and mighty,' so she had to switch her pronunciation between home and school. 'Ain't' was the most important word- at school it was a sin, but to not use it at home when talking to her neighbours would get her badly thought of. She soon became very adept at her verbal camouflage. She didn't dare practise her French at home; she was supposed to repeat all the French vowels like a goldfish. It always made her laugh when they did it in class; at home they would have ridiculed her mercilessly. But persevere she did with her piles of homework when the living room table was free from dinner and ironing, in the room with faded light which now also housed her eldest sister Betty's husband and baby (they slept on the sofa) and her mum and dad's pride and joy, her long awaited, baby brother Paul. Even though she did her best to switch her pronunciation, her childhood friends thought she was avoiding them because she was 'too stuck up' now. She wasn't, but she had to get two buses home and had piles of homework when she could get a seat in the house. They didn't seem to do any homework at Foxford secondary modern school where her sisters went. They also had boys there. Shirley's ears were very attentive when her elder sister Jean talked about Roy Allen. She said that Shirley might see him if she helped her with her paper round at the weekend.

School improved immensely when Shirley made two nice friends; Mary, the girl that she had saved from the worm and Jose. Jose invited her back to meet her parents and have tea after school. She went home happier than she had been for months, looking forward to the paper round the next morning, Saturday - would she catch a glimpse of *him?*

She enjoyed the guided tour, finding out where Roy lived and hearing about his brother's boxing success, but in the early hours of the paper round didn't see anybody much and her wellies were now getting too small and rubbed her feet. She was glad to get back home and sink into the worn but comfy sofa with her feet in a bowl of warm water.

A knock at the door and her mum let two very uncomfortable, red faced girls in - Jose and Mary.

'You forgot your school hat, and I didn't want you to worry or get in trouble on Monday,' Jose muttered in the doorway to a crowded room of people, watched by an equal sized crowd of grubby street children. 'It's okay,' she continued, 'you don't need to get up we can't stay - got dancing lessons, bye bye.'

Shirley was mortified. They couldn't have come at a worse moment; her feet in a bowl, Betty changing the baby's smelly nappy. How she suddenly hated her house, her life. Her family tried to calm her down, told her not to be a snob, but *they* didn't have to live this double life, she had tried *so* hard to fit in at school. She'd never have any friends now that they'd seen how she lived. Betty offered her a bacon sandwich, normally it would have cheered her up; she'd do almost anything for a bacon sandwich - but she was far too upset even to eat.

Her legs were really heavy as she approached the school gates on Monday morning, she had tried to say that she was sick and did feel sick but her elder sister said that it was best if she got it over with:

'You may feel like dying with shame but you don't die. If they're real friends they'll still be friends Shirl.'

Betty was always there for her, she had been clever enough to go to grammar school but hadn't. She was dainty with black hair and bright blue eyes – really pretty. In the war she had been in the land army and a German POW had taken a shine to her. After the war had ended he had arrived at her doorstep in a very smart car, but her mother had asked her to get rid of him before her dad saw him. She had now married a friendly Irishman and they were living and sleeping in the Thompson family living room/kitchen/washroom with their baby daughter whilst they were on the council list for a pre-fab.

Well to Shirley's amazement and delight, her friends Mary and Jose *were* true friends. They sensed how embarrassed she felt and were even kinder to her. They were really excited about something. So excited that they both spoke at the same time but Shirley got the gist of what they were saying:

'Look what we've got – they're autograph books. We've got one for you as well Shirley. We could go after the matinee and wait for all the famous ballerinas to come out of the theatre.'

'We might meet Norma Shearer or Alicia Markova.'

Life was worth living again.

Her two friends were quite different in character; Jose

loved dressing up and fashion, especially short skirts; she was blonde, bubbly and fun. Shirley was surprised that her parents were in the Salvation Army. Together they would design clothes, a yard of material and they could make a short skirt. Mary was dark haired, much quieter and went to church and loved ballet. Shirley regularly went to their houses and would draw fashionable clothes or ballerina costumes for them. Her designs included a lot of wedding and bridesmaid dresses; she had the most beautiful wedding planned in detail for herself.

She often took these two close friends to visit her own grandmother, her dad's mother who still lived in the centre of Coventry. Shirley was really proud of Granny Thompson who was not rich but would give them money to fetch chips from the chip shop and sweets and show them the portrait of her husband in his army uniform with all his medals, long since resting in the Flanders poppy fields. Granny had brought up her three children on her own and now suffered from rheumatoid arthritis, but always made Shirley and her friends welcome. Not only the friends from grammar school. As a young child Shirley had turned up with ragged, snotty-nosed friends who had also been treated to the best china and chip shop chips and made to feel special.

Mary even started to visit Shirley at home. They loved taking Shirley's baby brother, Paul, walks, practising their mothering skills on him.

As soon as they were old enough, Shirley and Jose got a Saturday job at Woolworths. At first Shirley unluckily got on the paint counter with a very large woman who kept sending her down a lot of steps to fetch heavy tins of paint, but as soon as the opportunity arose she got onto sweets and milkshakes with Jose, which was much more fun; and, earning money was marvellous. She voluntarily gave her mother her 10s 6d wages every other week. With the alternate week's money she was able to go with her friends to the ballet and see performances such as Swan Lake and get all the star performer's autographs – it was all so exciting. Then in the school summer holidays they'd go swimming at the baths. Jose would swim up and down the length of the pool while she and Mary had races mainly on the widths, both being about equal weak swimmers.

Shirley still managed to put some money aside; although it was warm in July and August, she knew that she would need a coat to start back for the final school year. Her figure had developed almost overnight and her coat wouldn't button up at all. She had finally become accepted at school and been voted the girl with the best figure in the school by the other girls, and had started to take a real pride in her appearance. She had seen a coat that she really wanted, a black teddy boy coat with a velvet collar. She had been trying it on in the shop for a few weeks, marvelling at how it looked and felt and putting money aside – it would be her first *new* coat.

***

Mary had some really exciting news for her friends:

'My parents have said that I'm to ask you *both* to come camping with us. We're going to Perranporth in

Cornwall. It'll be the best holiday *ever* all together.'

Well Shirley had a dilemma. It was very tempting, she'd never been camping or on holiday, only the odd day trip to the seaside, and it would be great fun with her friends.......but the coat!

She only just had enough money saved up for the coat. It was an agonising decision... but finally the coat won and her friends went on holiday without her.

She missed them that week, but went to get the coat. She couldn't resist wearing it even though it wasn't yet cold enough.

As she strutted along the Coventry high street in her new coat, Shirley spotted a billboard outside a newsagents; the headline made her stop and go cold.........:

'COVENTRY GIRL DROWNED AT SEA!'

Shirley's horrible intuition was correct....... poor Mary never came back from the holiday.

Jose, the stronger swimmer survived the current – just!

Shirley was a weaker swimmer than Mary, she was lucky that she never went on the holiday.

But she didn't feel lucky. The coat became a funeral coat!

She started the autumn school term sitting on her own in the classes that she would have sat in with Mary. She found herself crying in class unable to concentrate on the lessons. She was beside herself with grief for her quiet, kind, lovely friend. Grief turned to illness as she got severe tonsillitis and was booked into hospital to have them removed.

In the days after the operation, she was given jelly and ice- cream and felt some comfort from the sick little children who sat on her bed. Still, she couldn't face the thought of returning to school without Mary. What was the point anyway? She liked the subjects that she had chosen, architecture and artists through the ages, but there was no way *she'd* be going to art school or university.

From a young age she'd written all her own school letters, her mum always asked her to. She now put the skill to good use.

She wrote a letter to the Director of Education for the Midlands asking for her release from school stating:

> '…we need her out for financial reasons.' signed '*Walter Thompson.*'

Chapter 18.

STRIKING A MATCH!

Now nearly sixteen years old, a new chapter of Shirley's life began. No longer a school girl and now looking for a job. It wasn't difficult to find one, jobs were plentiful especially in Coventry with a booming car industry. At home it was expected that a large part of wages were handed over but if you were unhappy with a job you could get another the same day before returning home. Shirley was looking forward to having more money of her own and joining in more with her neighbours. Maybe it would help her stop grieving for Mary, take her mind off it all. She readily agreed when a girl in the street suggested that she came to their place and learnt to use a capstan.

It was an oily, repetitive factory job, but Shirley persevered and did well with the piece work, getting good bonuses and occupying her thoughts with the lovely clothes that she could buy and her cinema trips.

Her school days and artistic talents very soon became a distant dream.

Her mother wasn't happy though. Alice wasn't materialistic or ambitious. She knew that finding a husband was the main career of women but was upset that her bright, intelligent daughter was cooped up in a factory all day doing the same job as some who hadn't even learned to read. Shirley was in demand writing job applications and love letters for her peers but seemed to have lost her own sparkle.

She was surprised when her mother eagerly told her of a new vacancy that wouldn't pay so much:

'…but it'll be a much better job for you Shirl, I know you can do it. Now take tomorrow morning off and get smartened up and get down the garage down the road.'

She was surprised by her mother's persuasiveness; Alice rarely interfered. It wasn't a job that she'd have thought of applying for knowing little about cars and she certainly wouldn't have taken a day off work. She thought she was pleasing everyone with her earnings

224

and fitting in better and helping mind her little brother, Paul, in her spare time; but her mother really wanted her to try for this.

Alice even supervised her getting ready, finishing off her hair, rubbing it with a silk scarf to make it shine.

'Now don't be nervous, you've got nothing to lose by trying.'

'But I know nothing about garages and cars.'

'Well just be your old self and tell them what a quick learner you are, now let me see that lovely smile.'

Shirley thought her mum's expectations were misguided but had never disobeyed. Anyway it was nice to get dressed up and have a day off from the boring factory, so she happily strolled down to the garage to get the interview over with.

The garage owner was a bit unsure. She was very young and knew nothing about cars and garages, then one of the young apprentices winked at her. She blushed and smiled. Wow what a smile, what a looker, and she'd got class – she'd have the customers rolling in.

He wasn't wrong about the customers. But if he thought her incapable he had a pleasant surprise. She enthusiastically threw herself into the job. She insisted on getting under the cars and proudly jacking them up. The financial side was a piece of cake and she took over a lot of the bookwork. Her sparkly outgoing personality quickly returned, fuelled by compliments and whistles from the male customers. She loved her job and life was once again, not just for getting through, but for living.

Her wages, after paying her board, were spent on building up her wardrobe to copy her film star idols; satin, figure hugging, Miss Saigon style dresses with a slit up the side set off with stilettos. Stockings weren't always possible but gravy browning on her smooth long legs and a line drawn down the back with an eye pencil completed the act.

She no longer had to pay for the cinema or theatre, hopefuls queued up to take her and the more she insisted on friendship only, in her flirty make up and clothes, the more the young men insisted on taking her.

She would go pillion on a young man's new moped for a milk-shake in town, then get back to catch the bus to the cinema with another.

Only sometimes she missed the start of some of the films because she refused to get on the bus at the bus stop outside the Longford skating rink until she had seen a certain Roy Allen come out of his brother's skating rink. She knew the approximate time and if he was late she would make her escort wait for the next bus.

Every time she came close to him her confidence crashed and her body went as red as her hair. She thought it was no wonder he never approached her. She had seen him in the rink chatting and laughing with others. His brother, Les, had bought the rink with the money he had made at boxing. She was sure Roy had noticed her with his cool blue-grey eyes, but unlike most young men, he never approached her. Maybe he thought she was too young, maybe he thought she looked like a carrot the way she kept blushing. These thoughts were still flashing through her mind at the cinema when the leading lady on screen asked the handsome beau for a light for her cigarette…sultrily, seductively! Shirley's eyes shone as a plan formed in her head.

She bought some cigarettes and practised smoking. It was pretty horrible and choking at first. Everyone was surprised. They all smoked; it was considered cool and good for you but Shirley had said that it wouldn't fit in with her job at the garage. When she thought she had the hang of it, Greta Garbo style, she helped herself to a glass of her parent's sherry (another first), then walked apprehensively to Longford skating rink and waited in the foyer. As customary, Roy came out of the main skating area, tall, smartly dressed for a night on the town, his wavy hair bobbing on his forehead. Surprised to see her standing there with no male escort, he smiled. As his blue eyes embraced hers, Shirley's confidence died but she managed to mutter:

'Have you got a light please - I've forgotten my matches,' as her trembling hand put a cigarette between her carefully painted red lips.

He took a box of matches out of his pocket, struck one and lit the cigarette in her mouth. He was so close to her, their eyes locked. Shirley puffed so that the end of the cigarette beamed red, then, well-practised, sophisticatedly took the cigarette from her pouting lips and, smiling with her whole face, spoke to him:

'Thank-you.'

'No problem.'

He smiled as he put the used matchstick back in the box and hurried out the exit.

She had planned this for weeks, and that was all he had said to her – 'No problem.' He clearly wasn't interested, she supposed he was late for his bus to town. Did he have a girlfriend there? She hadn't seen him with one. Why did this thought upset her so much when he couldn't even be bothered to speak to her? Shirley waited a bit so that she didn't bump into him outside, then, feeling sick, went home.

The next few weeks she broke off with her escorts and didn't go out socialising. She now knew how hurtful it felt to want someone and have no hope. She made the decision not to encourage her admirers. She poured her passionate feelings into writing her friends love letters for them.

However the customers at work were still chatting her up. One in particular just wouldn't give up. He wanted to take her for a spin in his sports car. It was very tempting. It would certainly help cheer her up and he was very likeable. After a few weeks she decided she wasn't going to ruin the rest of her life moping about over someone who wasn't even interested enough to talk to her.

The spin in the sports car turned into a whirlwind romance. He really was very likeable and good looking and a real high flier with his own business and made it clear that he adored her. She wanted for nothing and was completely bowled over when after a few weeks of courting he turned up with a really dazzling diamond ring and asked her to be his fiancé. She was speechless and proudly wore the ring, the envy of her sisters and friends.

She was really starting to enjoy life again. But the engagement had raised expectations. He was planning to marry her; he was really good to her. She did want to marry, although not yet. She idolised her baby brother but wanted a career more than children. He said he understood and would be happy with as long an engagement as she wanted ….. but he now expected more than a quick kiss! And that was the problem – it just didn't feel right. However pleasant a night they had Shirley could not bring herself to go all the way. He was so nice, she worried that she was frigid, it just didn't feel right.

Fate decided for her. Picking her up outside her house, he drove to a quiet lane. He had some important news to tell her. He sat sombrely and took a while to speak. Shirley couldn't imagine what could be the matter. The news was more shocking than she'd anticipated: He had: 'got someone else pregnant!'

Shirley's legs turned to jelly at the news. She stared at him in horror. Eventually she spoke tearfully:

'But I thought you *loved* me.'

'I do Shirl, it's your fault; you kept sending me home all worked up and she was there waiting for me, begging for it…please, please forgive me!'

She gave him his answer – a diamond ring hit him, wack, between his eyes.

Alice watched her daughter mooch around the house for a few evenings after work then spoke out:

'Jean wants someone to go out with tonight. Get yourself ready, it'll do you good.'

'I'm not in the mood mam, not tonight.'

'Come on, stop feeling sorry for yourself, he's not worth it, you're well rid. Think of your sister.'

Shirley was surprised. Her mother hadn't been impressed with the car and flash ring and she was surprised herself that she didn't feel that upset. She knew that her elder sister Jean had her eye on a young man who frequented the nearby pub and would be glad of someone to accompany her. Well why not, her mother was right her ex wasn't worth losing sleep over and her sister had been sympathetic when Shirley had expected her to smirk because Shirley had flaunted her ring quite a bit. Yes she decided that she'd tag along but it was going to be a long time before she'd bother with men again. Only seventeen but had had enough of men and found out that she was frigid, she'd clearly have to concentrate on her career. These thoughts troubled her head as she mechanically got ready to go out. Without sparkle, without repeatedly checking in the mirror, she slipped her blue satin, figure hugging, mandarin dress over her nubile body. A quick brush of her long auburn hair and a pair of stilettos and she was ready to go.

'Shirley wait!'

Her mum stopped her going out the door and ran and fetched a bright red lipstick. She rubbed a bit into Shirley's cheeks with her finger, then wiped it with a handkerchief so that it just gave a slight pink glow, then carefully painted Shirley's mouth.

'There, that's better. You don't normally forget your lipstick. I hope you've remembered to put your knickers on; it's windy out,' she joked.

They all laughed. Alice's small kindnesses comforted and cheered everyone, especially her girls.

It's not easy to walk on uneven cobbles in stilettos even if you're well practised but luckily their destination wasn't far. The 'Engine' pub was a friendly, wholesome place, with bright brasses and a garden backing onto the Coventry canal. The girls were glad to get inside, out of the wind, welcomed by the warm, glowing fire.

Shirley was surprised to see Jean's friend Carol there, sitting near the fire. She'd been conned – she wasn't really needed at all. Carol welcomed her warmly. Shirley had filled in an application form for a job for Carol who hadn't learnt to read and Carol had got the job then been promoted.

'I'm buying the drinks tonight,' Carol insisted. 'What are you drinking Shirl?'

'Orange juice, please.'

'You can have what you want, you look old enough.'

'No really I like orange juice best.'

Shirley had only had a few sups of her drink when Jean commanded:

'Drink up quick, I'm getting the drinks.'

There at the bar buying his drink was Mike, smartly dressed in a suit. Shirley stopped breathing as she recognized his friend.

Jean took her glass.

'Sherry, please Jean – a double.'

Carol looked at her puzzled but Jean understood. She remembered a few years previously Shirley helping her on a paper round early in the morning just so that she could interrogate her about Mike's friend - Roy Allen, who had been at her high school - Foxford.

Jean returned with two drinks including a schooner of sherry.

'I hope you don't mind, Mike's bought me a drink and asked me to sit with them. You can come if you like.'

'No, we're okay, we've got loads to catch up on. You go ahead.'

Shirley had just become very conscious that her hair was windswept and she hadn't put her mascara on and thought a sherry would help.

The night seemed to go on forever. She thought of the meeting with the matchstick which she now resembled sitting by the fire drinking sherry after sherry. She wasn't going over unless *he* invited her and there was no chance of that; he'd practically raced out of the door that night she asked him for a light. He seemed to keep glancing at her but quickly looking away as she caught him. He still made her heart beat faster.

The girls drank up as last orders were called and took their glasses to the bar.

'Mike's giving us a lift home.' Jean informed them.

'Thanks but it's okay, I'll walk, I need some fresh air.' Shirley really did need some fresh air.

'I'll take *you* home.'

Roy's beautiful blue-grey eyes looked into hers, pleadingly.

She wasn't cross that he hadn't asked properly, his eyes said more. They said that it had taken him all night and a lot of alcohol to say that.

Maybe, just maybe she hadn't been mistaken that the deep longing was reciprocal. She stopped breathing and just nodded.

Out in the night air, she shivered. Roy gently put his long, warm gangster style coat on her and buttoned it up, then with a big smile his trilby. Her smile filled her face as he looked lovingly into her eyes.

The coat came right down to her shoes.

'I feel like Bonny and Clyde,' she joked.

'Well we can rob a bank another night if you want but you've had a lot more to drink tonight than you normally have, so let's get you back to Lady Lane safe. Hold onto my arm.'

He knew where she lived and that she normally had orange juice. Her prying questions revealed that he knew almost everything about her.

He'd felt in awe of her because she went to the grammar school.

'I went to Oxford,' he informed her, 'without the 'F.'

The beer had really loosened his tongue, he was really chatty and fun. Before they knew it they were outside her front door, much too soon. She didn't want the magic to end, neither did he.

She had waited so long for this it was like two magnets trying to part, she spoke what they were both thinking:

'Shall we stay out a bit longer I'm not ready to go in yet.'

He took her arm again and they walked back up the lane. As they passed the churchyard they both instinctively knew they wanted to be alone somewhere secluded, just the two of them, the moon and the stars. They felt as if they had been together all of their life. But Shirley just had to voice her concern.

'Maybe all this is the drink talking when you were sober and I asked you for a light you didn't want to know me, you weren't interested.'

'Yes but you weren't dressed up as a gangster then,' he teased. 'I was so surprised to see you standing there; it just threw me. I turned to come back in, but I hadn't put the match out properly when I put it back in the match-box and the box burst into flames in my pocket. I burnt my trousers and all my

239

fingers and had to go home.'

His words hit Shirley like a thunderbolt. Lips slightly ajar she looked deep into his eyes. Then she laughed as she imagined the vision of him jumping about on fire, no longer cool and aloof; and he laughed. Her really euphoric laugh was from the overwhelming realisation that he had felt as she had. He laughed with relief because at long last he had managed to tell her of his feelings for her. Together they stopped laughing as their eyes fused together, sending delicious electric currents throughout their bodies. As their lips touched, they melted into one, into.....another world. Their minds and bodies oblivious to everything save their passion.

Chapter 19.

OBLIVION.

Shirley awoke to the sound of beautiful birdsong. What a wonderful dream. She was lying wrapped in the strong, warm arms of the one she loved. It was so real. She opened her eyes.....it **was** real. And... it was dawn and she hadn't been home, and she'd got work!!! Like one synchronised being, they woke together. She returned Roy's coat and hat. He gave her one more strong, embracing kiss before she ran off in her tight dress on her jelly legs, holding her stilettos.

Inside her home, she had a big problem. To get to her bedroom she had to go up the creaky stairs and pass through her parent's bedroom, then get in bed with her sisters. Her dad would kill her if he knew that she'd come in this late. Only one thing to do – stay up and pretend she'd got up early. She'd had a bit of sleep and felt ecstatically awake, alive; her eyes sparkled, a dreamy contented smile was etched on her pink

241

tinged face.

Her mind intoxicated with excitement, more exhilarated than on a fair rollercoaster; it was the highest swing that she wanted to stay on forever.

She didn't manage to act very normal when her mother got up to make up the coal fire; she just couldn't shake off the dopey smile.

Alice hadn't seen her daughter like this since she had won the raffle at the bike race.

'Tell me about it quick Shirl, before the others get up.' Holding a newspaper over the fireplace to draw the fire, Alice was insistent.

Shirley elatedly told her mother that her childhood idol had kept her out all night. Alice lost her focus on hearing the disturbing news; the newspaper on the fire burst into flames. She prodded it down with the poker, black burnt bits of paper and soot wafted over her anguished face.

'Shirl, you can't court him. He goes round with a load of gangsters.'

Alice was really worried. She listened to the boxing on the radio and had followed Roy's brother's boxing career with enthusiasm. But she had also listened to the street gossip. Fame had brought a wide spectrum of associates to the Allen household. Some famous as the comedian 'Tommy Trinder' who had toured South Africa with Les and stayed at the Allen's council house. Others wanting to be part of the act included some who'd served prison sentences. All were made welcome at the Allen household indiscriminately.

'But *he's* not a gangster mam. He's so loving and kind and … caring.'

She had that dazed look again.

'Well he won't think much of you, staying out all night with him when he's only just bothered with you. I can't believe you've done that; not when you've been brought up respectable. You'd better put a bit of this soot on your dress: it'll give you an excuse to go upstairs and get some more suitable work clothes on.'

The hailstone of words hit Shirley hard!

The workday seemed so long and fraught with mistakes. Alcohol and lack of sleep were easy enemies compared with the terror which now attacked her. His kisses had been so full of love, but he was a man. He must think her a cheap trollop. He hadn't arranged to meet her again. Had she let the alcohol deplete her common sense? Ensnaring a man required tactics. She was an expert at manipulating young admirers, but he was the only one that she had ever really, really wanted and she had blown it. She knew her mother was right to say what she did. But the feeling between them....the uncontrollable magic. Had he felt it?

That evening at home, she couldn't eat her dinner. She had never not eaten her dinner. She'd better not go out looking for him. She would look more of a trollop. She felt ill. But she had to try and look as normal as possible.

She did the washing up so that the Belfast sink was clear and washed her hair in cold water, then sat on the rug by the fire to dry. She had helped make the colourful rug. Her mum regularly sent her to jumble sales for cheap cloths with instructions to 'get as much red as you can.' If you stood by someone you knew who was serving you could get a large pile really cheaply. She loved scrambling among the busy crowd for bargains. Then, with her mum and sisters, she had cut the bits of cloth and pushed them through holes in a sack to make a warm multi-coloured hearth rug. It was useful to sit on tonight as the chairs and settee were all taken; but though the room was busy and full, Shirley was in her own little faraway place.

Whilst her hair was still damp, she curled it into little fossil shaped rings and pinned it with hairclips all over her head. When it dried and she removed the hairgrips it would be wavy. She needed to look her best tomorrow in case she accidentally bumped into *him*. She made up a greyish paste with some fuller's earth and a little water and smeared it over her face.

Her mother answered the knock at the door to the smart, handsome young man dressed in trench coat and trilby. She didn't have to ask:

'Shirl, someone to see you.'

Roy's eyes followed Alice's gaze to the other end of

the room. The sight was quite shocking; not merely how many people were in such a shabby room, but his beautiful red head had short hair. She must wear a wig.

Shirley couldn't open her mouth to speak properly, not just through the shock of seeing him there. Her mind not functioning properly, she had left the paste on too long and by the hot fire the mask had over-hardened.

She spoke like an inept ventriloquist, without moving her lips.

'Tell im im oshing iy hair.'

'She's having a night in washing her hair,' Alice was pleased to explain.

Once again Roy was full of dutch courage. He couldn't face her without a few drinks and was determined. He also didn't want to lose face in front of his friend. He had worried all day that she might get into trouble and she might think he'd taken advantage of her, so he was out to make amends and impress her. He had asked one his friends to chauffeur them so that he could take her out in style. Alice was horrified to see a gangster style car complete with Italian- looking driver outside the house.

'I really need to speak to her please, Mrs Thompson, I'll wait outside.'

Roy was disappointed that she wasn't ready to come out. Still he had seen her with quite a few escorts and heard that she messed them around. The wig was a bit of a shock too, but he decided that it didn't change his feelings. He knew he wouldn't cope with her going out with others. He would end up killing someone.

Eventually, she appeared from the house looking so beautiful, complete with long wavy auburn hair.

His inner turmoil surfaced quite abruptly.

'You need to make your mind up. If you want to be my girl, there'll be no messing me about with other men and washing your hair excuses.'

If anyone else had spoken to her like that, she'd have blitzed them.

But there was such a connection of real deep feeling

between them that all she heard was his love for her.

Her eyes smiled lovingly at him as she spoke:

'I'll get my coat.'

She couldn't resist a small tease:

'Bye mum, we're just off to rob a bank.'

***

Shirley had thought that she had been happy in life but now it seemed that her life had been grey and was suddenly in colour. She felt so deeply loved, so wanted and special.

This wasn't without its drawbacks; she thought Roy was going to hit an admirer who chatted her up and she had to quickly curb her flirtatious nature, but it didn't really matter because she wasn't interested in other men and now felt complete without attention seeking.

Roy didn't mean to be so jealous, but he was a bit insecure, and he was besotted with her.

His family were surprised; he hadn't been very

bothered about girls before and had always been there 100% for them. He let Les go to London without him; he'd never done that before. The family were really shocked when he didn't go to watch his brother fight Terry Downes at Earles Court, London. Roy had *never* missed a big fight and this was an important top class fight. Terry Downes was nicknamed 'The Paddington Express' for his aggressive fighting style. It was to be a really big match; they called it 'Rumble in the Jungle.' His uncle Peter called at the house with a last minute attempt to whiz him there in a car and still he wouldn't go. Les won the sensational fight against Terry Downes who went on to become World champion.

Roy hadn't meant to miss this fight but had forgotten to tell Shirl that he wasn't calling for her. She hadn't got a telephone and when his uncle Peter turned up last minute to take him, he couldn't bring himself to leave her waiting not knowing where he was.

The family thought she had bewitched him.

When he told Shirley she said she would have

understood, known that it must be something important. He needed even more assurance of her love for him and his self- worth than she did. He was surprised but pleased when she said that she was glad Blackie their chauffeur had gone as well. It would be nice to have him all to herself.

November wasn't a good month to be without a car. Out walking in the fields a sudden downpour drenched them. Roy led them to a disused railway wagon and managed to prise it open. They clambered in for shelter. Shirley had a coat on but her hair was dripping wet:

'Take your wig off, bab. I don't mind I love you.'

'Wig? What wig?' She saw his serious face –

'You *are* joking?'

'I saw your short hair in the house, it's okay honestly.'

She laughed - he was so lovely.

'I had my hair pinned up. Here pull it – it's all

real….. Do you need glasses?'

'Probably, when I had measles as a child my eyesight in my right eye was damaged by looking at a bright light above my bed. It was never the same after, but cos I'd seen Les being beat up for wearing glasses, I never told anyone. I couldn't see the blackboard at school very well. I failed my driving test, cos of my eyesight as well.'

Shirley's motherly instinct was kindled:

'Here your shirts wet take it off, we'll hang it up to dry.'

He shook his head:

'I'm okay.'

'I know you've got boils on your back. I've felt them. They'll go quicker if you take your shirt off more. Don't be embarrassed with me. I love you… and your boils.'

They spent many blissful hours in the derelict railway wagon throughout the winter. Together they undressed their innermost secrets, their bodies and their souls. Shirley felt that she needed nothing to make her blissfully happy except him.

She was surprised when he called for her in a lorry.

'It's my works lorry. Don't worry Shirl - I drive it all the time at work.'

'I'm surprised they let you when you haven't passed your test.'

'Baz, the driver has broken his arm but he's passed his test so I drive it for him, with him in the passenger seat. I drive it all round the country. I'm a good driver Shirl! I thought it'd be nice for you to have a change. Where do you want to go first?'

He *was* a good driver and wanted to share that with her.

They cruised around in the lorry a bit then realized that they wouldn't be able to get up the lane and over the fields to their railway carriage or their church yard. They needed to find somewhere new for their courting. Roy knew just the place.

The Slough at Wyken, Coventry was a lake surrounded by fields, a busy boating lake by day but that evening, wonderfully desolate.

It was so romantic, sitting high up in the warm lorry cab; looking out over the lake, lit gently by the moon and the stars... the World to themselves.

Roy clambered over to the passenger seat to put his strong arm around her, hold her. He commented on their lovely view; as he spoke, he thought the view of her, sitting there so happy was even lovelier; the most beautiful view that he had ever seen. He couldn't resist kissing her. The fire from his lips quickly flickered throughout her love-parched body, creating a firestorm of passion. All that existed was each other.

Pure ecstatic, pleasure filled every part of their being. Shirley felt the delightful hot flushes of love - except her feet were wet...very wet.

The lorry had slipped into the lake.

Roy had borrowed the works lorry without permission or a driving licence - he *had* to get it out!

Somehow, many hours later, after much wading in muddy water and putting rocks under the wheels, the lorry became mobile and they could laugh and joke about him taking her on a cruise. Nothing blighted their happiness when they were together.

It was the next morning, nearly time to go to work when Shirley was delivered home. She'd been late quite a lot just lately as they totally kept losing track of time, but tonight she couldn't just stay up and pretend she'd got up early, not wet and covered in mud. Her clean clothes were upstairs. She slowly climbed the creaking stairs and tip-toed into the girl's bedroom, but she was seen. Her dad wasn't asleep. He'd overheard her sisters and mother secretly discussing her new behaviour.

The following day after work, despite the lack of sleep, Shirley was nearly ready to go out when her dad returned home.

He confronted her with the hearsay and his fears but got no reply.

'You needn't think you're going anywhere tonight

young lady. I'm not having this behaviour any longer. You're grounded until I decide otherwise.'

'You can't do that to me dad. I'm not a child any more. I go to work. I've got someone who cares about me a lot more than you ever did. I'll do as I please!' and she brushed back her hair, defiantly.

Wally was taken aback, nobody in the house had challenged his authority before. He had been oblivious to the anarchy that had built up in his daughter's head; she had always been so eager to please him. The anarchy had started with the sandwiches: Shirley had discovered, before she started work and earned her own money, that a tiny bit of meat sneaked off each of her dad's work sandwiches would make *her* a delicious sandwich.

Wally felt that he was doing this for her own good and not sure how to handle it. Usually the threat of his belt was enough to command total obedience. He'd never had to use it on her. He took it off threateningly:

'You'll feel my belt if you don't get up those stairs right now, young lady!'

He took a few steps towards her, 'wack' she bashed his bryl creamed head with the hairbrush. Alice started shouting at him pleadingly:

'Don't hit her Wal, don't hit her!'

Roy had recently arrived and heard the commotion. He opened the door and, in a voice not to be argued with, commanded:

'**Don't touch her Wally**! Come on Shirl, *you're coming home with me*!'

Chapter 20.

TO HAVE AND TO HOLD.

Shirley felt so relieved by Roy's strong protectiveness, but worried – had he heard the full argument? He was walking so fast that she couldn't keep up with him. She hadn't even noticed herself that her period was late, let alone know that her family were discussing it. Round the corner of the street he stopped and asked her:

'Is it true, what they were saying?'

He looked worried to death. It hadn't really crossed his mind either. He was only just twenty years old and hadn't really thought seriously about .....well, anything serious.

Everything had been instinct, even just, when he felt the need to save her, not only from her father's anger but the disgust that he felt about her living in such a cramped hovel. Nobody should live like that, but especially not someone so clever, so talented, so wonderful. But this was really **not** what he planned. He had just been enjoying himself. He hadn't saved or worked at his career. This was definitely not what he planned for her, for them.......for *all* of them!

She knew by his quietness and the deep heavy frown lines that he was deeply disturbed. But as he looked down at her, so vulnerable and worried, yet still so beautiful, he managed to say in an adult, reassuring way:

'Don't worry, you don't have to worry – I'm gonna look after you.'

She'd heard this 'don't worry' a few times before; it had regularly got her home late, stranded in a lake, possibly pregnant and now unable to go home; but as always, and especially now, she *felt* reassured and filled with happiness.

Shirley hadn't been able to take friends home much:

'What will your parents say when I just turn up?'

He laughed: 'That's what everyone does at our house.

We've always got loads of visitors. I wish you'd seen some of the visitors our Les's brought home; famous people, comedians, coloured people from the Gold Coast that he spars and boxes with, people who've been in prison. I bet me mum'll be pleased to see what you look like, she's been asking questions about you.'

***

It was true Roy, like all the family, had always been able to just turn up with friends and Maud had always made them feel at home, but this was different. Maud adored her children and when it came to partners had such high aspirations for them. She was worried that Roy was no longer mixing much with his family or getting much sleep, or bothering with his career. She was curious about the young woman that she had heard was from the slummy part of 'Lady Lane' and worse - had been seen flirting with a string of men, and now seemed to be bewitching her beloved son. He had always been impulsive, sometimes reckless and driven by his heart, but he had never shocked and horrified her as much as he did when he came home that night:

259

'Mam, I'm home,' he called from the hall. Appearing in the kitchen he did the introductions:

'This is Shirl….. she's come to live here.'

He squeezed the hand of the young girl in the Chinese prostitute-like clothing with black mascara running down her young face. 'She can sleep with me, we're going to get married one day.'

Maud had the same feeling that she got when a German bomb had dropped near their house.

She looked at his proud face, squeezing the little floozy's hand tightly.

Eventually, after what seemed like ages to Shirley who was going redder and redder, she nodded thoughtfully and spoke:

'She can sleep in Julie's bed with our Julie.'

***

Maud didn't usually judge people harshly with unsympathetic, moral principles. It was only because of her overwhelming motherly love and idolisation of her offspring. Indeed young Julie, still at school, wasn't really Roy's sister, she was his niece but she had been born at Stratford in an unmarried mother's institution to his eldest sister Sheila. The father, an American G.I. had disappeared to America unknowing. Many in this situation had no choice but to have their baby's heartbreakingly taken away from them and adopted. Maud, had adopted Julie and her other daughter Joyce's little Albert, when Joyce got married at a young age, then divorced.

She apportioned no blame or shame to her daughters but reasoned that it was the result of: the war climate of not knowing if you were going to live another day (Joyce had even had a tooth broken by debris from a nearby bomb explosion); the lack of contraception available; and that her daughters were *so pretty*.

She raised the two family additions with the same unconditional love as she gave her own and was as close as any mother could possibly have been. When, at a young age, Julie had to go away to an institution run by catholic nuns in Coleshill for several years because of a problem with her hip, Maud never missed the allowed weekly visit, even if it meant walking miles.

Shirley had heard of Maud's fearless loyalty to her children many years before. Her sister Christine came home from school upset that Albert, (Roy's younger adopted brother) kept pinching her. Shirley offered to go up to the school to sort it out, knowing that her own parent's shied away from such things. Christine had told her that it was no use as 'that woman will only come up and tell them it's not her son's fault and nothing'll get done; she won't hear a bad word said about her kids.' In all likelihood young Albert, who then grew up to be very kind hearted, probably liked Christine and was showing it in a typical but horrid boyish way.

Julie's initial reaction to this person that she didn't know sleeping with her wasn't welcoming, but there was no way Maud was going to let an unmarried couple sleep together so that was the only place available.

Shirley also got a cool reception from Roy's elder

sisters who were very close to their mother and only wanted the best for their brother. It wouldn't be easy to win them over; without knowing her, they had formed a very strong opinion.

To Shirley's delight, Roy introduced her to the family menagerie. He had a golden whippet-like dog 'Cinders' that had been the runt of a litter of stray dogs that were found with their mother under a bus that was snowed in. She was quiet, clingy and trembly, like a little deer. Then the budgie 'Joey', that said a lot and 'Turk,' the Alsatian dog, fierce looking at first sight but kind, intelligent and so loyal when you got to know him. Along with Jack-russels and ferrets for rabbiting, there was a lot of work to do with the animals; Shirley started straight away, feeding and grooming them. The busy householders were glad of this help, especially the animals. Turk and Cinders began to follow Shirley around, supportively as if they sensed her need.

After the first night, she suggested that Roy go out with his family without her:

'I haven't fetched any clean clothes to go out and you haven't spent much time with your family, it'll do you good and I can get to know Julie better.'

**

The two girls sat in the back room. They lit some candles and got the fire roaring and some dandelion and burdock pop. Sitting with dogs on their laps and the budgie swearing and making them laugh, the girls warmed to one another. Shirley found Julie very friendly and witty and chatty, and she learnt a lot about Roy's past. She was starting to recover from the recent trauma and relax and enjoy herself when she heard.....a horrible deep moan, followed by an even louder one The two girls were on their own in the house. Then, through the candle- lit window they saw a large hand. It slid down the dark window pane.... slowly, accompanied by another deep moan. The two girls were petrified.

Finally, together, with the dogs, they switched the electric lights on and made their way to the back door. Peeping through a tiny crack in the door, they could see a *body* slumped on the floor.

Julie started to laugh, heartily… the laughter of relief.

'Shirley, meet the man of the house, me dad Capel – looks like he's had one too many again.'

The other men of the Allen family, Albert, Don and Les were also very helpful and friendly and their spouses, were also very understanding and welcoming. The spouses included 'Boet,' -   Joyce's new husband. Shirley loved helping with their toddler Gary. It reminded her of her own brother Paul. Les no longer lived at home but with his lovely young wife 'Margaret', not far away, in Longford, and made her very welcome at their house adjoined to their off-licence. Margaret was especially glad of Shirley's help with learning to cook. The two of them had a lot of laughs leaving the giblets in a roast chicken and trying to get the lumps out of gravy. Women were expected to put on such a show of culinary expertise for their men.

Shirley was determined to make the best of it; especially as she was probably expecting a baby. Not wanting to be worse thought of, she and Roy hadn't informed the Allen family but decided to book their wedding. At least they might then be allowed to sleep together!

They didn't tell the family they were off to book their wedding, just that they were going to the cinema in Coventry to watch Norman Wisdom. They managed to book the wedding for a very special day, March 15th – Shirley's 18th birthday.

Then they bought the gold ring and laughed and hugged on the back row of the cinema, carefree and happy, as, with mouths full of fudge, they entered the hysterically funny world of the character Norman Pitkin.

***

They had to wait 3 weeks before the wedding. Shirley kept taking her ring out of its little box and trying it on. It was only a cheap one, as Roy had persuaded her to pack her garage job in and had lost his own job over the lorry incident. He said he'd get her a more expensive one when he got a well- paid job, but she knew that she would never want to change this gold band and the memory of that special day - the loving, proud look on his face as she tried on the gold band that would unite them forever. She couldn't wait to be married. She spent much less time with Roy on his own now. Family and friends seemed to be accompanying them everywhere. She was amazed at how many visitors came to the house, except for herself, everyone seemed to be welcome.

One day an old lady turned up at the door with a disabled daughter. Maud invited them in as always and cooked them a duck egg each while Shirley made a pot of tea. 'Old Gal Wells,' as everyone called her was a soothsayer. She was poor but never charged the Allen family. She offered to do a séance in the living room.

Curious, Shirley attended, sitting in a circle holding hands. Old Gal Wells's face contorted as she went trance - like, her voice high pitched. The message was for Shirley. Shirley's hair pricked up on her arms as Old Gal Wells said that she could see a woman standing behind her, who looked identical. She was holding two babies and shaking her head, telling Shirley to be careful.

Shirley had gone into the séance skeptical, but nobody there knew that her deceased Aunt Jayne was said to be the image of her, and she had still not told anyone of her missed period. It was eerie.

**

With the last of her money, Shirley had bought a new dress. It was black and white herringbone design and respectable looking. She looked really classy in it and stunning with her long shining hair. She so wanted to fit in and look the part for baby Kay's christening – Joyce and Boet's latest arrival. It was a real family day of rejoicing. She wondered if *she* would ever have this. Roy had now told everyone of their wedding plans but no-one had said much about their big day.

Just three days before the wedding, disaster struck!

A lady came to the house, claiming that she was from the health authority to see Roy Allen. If Roy had known who she was, he would have legged it.

His heart sank as she smirkingly said:

'Oh we've found you at last!'

She was actually from the armed forces. All healthy males not in coal mining, the royal navy or farming were expected to serve in the armed services on National Service, or (conscription as it was commonly called), for eighteen months. Many avoided it, especially if they had good jobs and were career training.

Roy had managed to avoid it for three years. His mother had sent letters back with *'address unknown'* on them. It seemed a horrible coincidence that they had now found him.

He protested that he was to be married, but his protests were unsuccessful; he was to report for duty in 'two weeks' – eleven days after the wedding day.

***

The wedding day arrived, Shirley's eighteenth

birthday. They had briefly discussed cancelling it with the change of circumstances. Roy was worried that he wouldn't be much of a provider, with his scant National Service pay, and would have liked her to have a really special day. But she still hadn't started her period and she would get a small married allowance as his wife, enough to pay her board at Maud's. As they looked at each other, they knew that they wanted to go ahead.

'Stop being silly, Roy, it'll be special to me whatever it's like – I'm marrying *you.*'

She didn't look especially weddingy, but Roy was proud of her in the dress she had worn to the christening and a fur coat that Margaret had kindly insisted on lending her. And he looked very handsome in a blazer and trousers, and very young, not yet twenty-one.

Boet drove them to the Coventry registrar office. He was to be a witness. They nearly missed the other witness as they looked for Shirley's sister 'Jean' along the Longford Road. She had been sitting in the courtyard of Longford Church – the reason made Shirley's day – her mother, who felt a bit giddy on the main road, accompanied her! Shirley had really missed her mother. She never went anywhere much, it meant a lot to Shirley to have her there, smiling with her large flowery button hole. Nobody else came; some had work, Maud and Joyce had flu. The Coventry registrar office was at the top of a building that looked derelict as it had been bombed and the repairs not completed.

***

After the ceremony, and confetti thrown over the married couple, the little group went to a nearby pub, where Roy bought a few rounds of drinks, only he and his new wife didn't have one. They made excuses, thanked everyone and left because really they couldn't afford a drink for themselves. Boet had to get back to work; Alice told them to pop in later and she'd make them a ham sandwich.

On the bus home Shirley saw a school colleague from Stoke Park, a reminder of the past, not long ago but seemed like a lifetime. She remembered her detailed drawings of her fabulous, romantic future wedding that her friends had admired.

'Shirley, it's wonderful to see you,' then, seeing the confetti enquired:

'Have you been to a wedding?'

'Yes… a friends.'

Shirley was very glad that her acquaintance got off at the next stop, as Roy had gone very quiet.

'Whos wedding?' he muttered.

She squeezed his hand:

'Well it wasn't how I'd planned it, but it's only one day and now I've got you. I wouldn't change you for a big posh wedding or… anything – ever!'

'One day I'll make it up to you… and get you a *really* expensive ring.'

She looked lovingly at the golden band on her finger.

'I'm *never* taking *this* off!'

Chapter 21.

ALONE AGAIN.

Back at the house Maud had a surprise for the newly-weds:

'We thought it'd be nice for you to have a bit of a honeymoon, a holiday…'

They looked at her hopefully.

'We've got some tents and everything. We're all going to Blackpool.'

'We?' Roy queried.

'Yes, it'll help me and Joyce get over this flu.' She saw his face: 'You'll have your own tent now you're married.'

The following day the convoy set off. Unfortunately March weather and Blackpool with poor quality tents was a bit of a disaster. Only one of the dilapidated tents stood up to the challenge. Undeterred, Maud had a very close friend who owned a guesthouse in Blackpool. The men shared the tent and Shirley spent most of her 'honeymoon' nights in a double bed with Joyce and Julie. Another tent was bought and, at Roy's insistence, she was able to sleep with her husband - but in a shared tent with Boet, Joyce and little Gary. She wouldn't have minded so much but time was running short. The tent was in a field quite a long way from the outside water tap so even washing was off the agenda. Despite her muddy appearance and rats tails hair, Roy still felt passionately in love with her, but he had to be content with just rubbing her frozen nose at night. As always they made the best of it. They only had a little money and went to the greyhound races with the others. Daringly, after a few races, Roy said that they might as well put all they had left on one greyhound, as there wasn't enough money left for another day out, and she could choose the dog. Roy groaned at the dog, she picked; she just liked the name. It didn't have much chance with those odds, but he didn't want to upset her, and she couldn't do any worse than he had; so he just hugged her and smiled. She'd never bet before but with beginners luck (well everyone has *some* luck!) - she *won* at twenty to one - enough money for the best of Blackpool pleasure beach, a meal out in style and a lot of beer and laughs.

***

They'd enjoyed the communal honeymoon but were desperate to be alone – time was moving too quickly.

Just 11 days after the wedding, 3 days after the 'honeymoon,' Les drove Roy, with Shirley clinging onto him, to Coventry railway station and instructed him:

'Don't start any fights or get into trouble.' He knew how reluctant Roy was to go, leaving his young bride.

Shirley cried inconsolably all the way back.

The feeling didn't change once the crying stopped. It was painful, like giving up an addiction or losing a body part.

She found some comfort in looking after the dogs. Turk, the large Alsatian, and trembly Cinders, became her firm companions, even sleeping under her bed at night. She started work at a local factory on a capstan again. This, she found hard as she had started to feel very tired and sick with the pregnancy but bound up her bump and carried on. Conscription wages were very poor and the money would help her to visit her beloved and save up for their own place. Back at the Allen house there was plenty to do in the evenings; Maud had decided to go back to Blackpool to help run the guesthouse. Shirley was left with a lot of men in the days when men weren't very domesticated. The sandwiches for work took two loaves. But she didn't complain; keeping busy was the best way to get through.

She toyed with the idea of leaving, but only briefly. This was Roy's home. She wanted to be here when he came home and if she left who knows what stories about her might emerge. At least they would all see that she was a good, faithful wife. She determined that nothing and no-one was going to break up their marriage.

She wasn't the only one having a hard time. Roy had

never written a letter before but now they came thick and fast about how miserable he felt without her, how much he missed and loved her.

He didn't put the full extent of his suffering in the letters, but some filtered through. His 21st birthday April 13th he spent:

'...crying all night......Don't worry I haven't gone soft. I was peeling onions in Jankers ALL night...'

Roy's 10 weeks training was at Stratford. He was assigned to the Pioneer Corps. This was the regiment where anyone expected to be insubordinate or difficult or illiterate was placed, though many were not from these pigeon holes. Learning to iron and polish, the hard physical training regime all day, and the torrential shouting, bullying and abuse from the corporals and sergeant majors was only part of it. The barrack conditions and food were austere with no privacy and the place was surrounded by barbed wire and guard dogs. This was largely to stop trainees from escaping. Young men from caring homes found it a real shock as they were banded in dormitories with dozens of others, some who had been in prison.

This didn't worry Roy – he was accustomed to defending himself and mixing with people from hard backgrounds and quickly made friends; but it was clear from very early on in his training that he was going to have a very, very hard time. Maybe his evident toughness and the contempt in his face for the pettiness, or his popularity, or that his brother was a boxer and he declined to join the boxing. He didn't really know why, but he was bullied brutally by those in charge. He tried really hard to comply, but even when he was right at the back of a parade, a sergeant shouted from the front that one of Roy's buttons wasn't polished. There was no way the sergeant could have seen from that position and the buttons were highly polished but there was no arguing, another night of jankers – scrubbing toilets with a toothbrush and peeling vegetables all night followed by another hard day of physical endurance.

Those in charge had a difficult job of training the reluctant men who had often left girlfriends, family, careers. Even parliament passed a motion in 1957 saying that it was going to end National Service which now seemed pointless and was hindering the country's workforce by conscripting so many young men. Maybe some of those in charge thought the harshness necessary to maintain order, and teach discipline... but some enjoyed bullying.

Somehow Roy got through the basic training and went home, for his first leave.

Shirley was shocked to see how thin he was – he looked like he'd been in an enemy prisoner of war camp. He was equally shocked; her pregnancy was showing well but her face was gaunt her eyes sunk into dark circles. The bright lipstick and rouge couldn't mask her suffering. She hadn't told him in her letters about her vomiting and how hard she'd been working. He would have made her pack her job in.

Everyone wanted to see Roy that day but as soon as it started to get dark he and Shirley made their excuses and went to bed...or at least they tried. Shirley got into bed first while Roy used the bathroom. He was met at the bedroom door by a fierce wolf-like dog growling and showing his teeth. At least someone was looking out for his wife. Shirley had to take Turk downstairs, let Roy in bed first and then follow with the dog. This worked, and they just held each other, silently, complete, the stresses of time ebbing away.

The next day Shirley wanted to go a walk. Roy wondered if she would manage it. The birth wasn't for another few months, but her bump was massive and her twig legs didn't look as they could support her.

They couldn't wait to be alone over their beloved fields.

'Better not go too far' he joked: 'I've learnt to iron and clean but not midwifery.'

Fate had been tempted. Strolling along, Shirley suddenly stopped. Colour drained from her face as she bent over with pain. Roy carried her back to the house.

She gave birth to a boy *and* a girl, but sadly they were too small. The girl was stillborn and the boy lived for a few hours in his mother's arms.

The deep grief which followed included a funeral with tiny coffins.

***

Still grieving and needing one another, Roy was forcibly taken back to the barracks, by the army and got 15 days in jankers for overstaying his leave. But now he was even more determined; she *needed* him!

'I'm going to get more leave, Shirl, and get out sooner, I promise!'

If she'd known *how* he was going to, she'd have tried to stop him. He applied to box for the army. He struggled through the qualifying bouts because his body was so emaciated but somehow he did qualify. From then on, the bullying stopped. He was given good food and more leave. Shirley started to visit him and stay weekends at Stratford. As he started to build up he was considered a match for the Malayan army champion. He was promised that he would get out earlier. The pain in the ring would be worth it.

Only the pain didn't end there. He hadn't been quite

ready and neither was the makeshift boxing ring. His head cracked on an unpadded concrete post......there was no shakily getting up before or after the count of ten. He lay...bleeding and unconscious.

He was still unconscious, in a coma when Shirley and his father arrived at the hospital in Liverpool. Capel supported Shirley as her legs gave way with the quietly spoken news from the doctor in the white coat:

'He may never gain consciousness. If he does it's likely that he'll have a changed personality and may not even know you or want to know you. We just don't know.'

Capel had to return home, but first he helped Shirley find a guesthouse. For several weeks, she sat by Roy's bed at visiting times, talking to him holding his hand. Between visiting times she cruised on the Mersey ferry, in her own lonely little bubble, not able to quite believe that the nightmare was real.

Would she wake up and it had all been a dream – *would he...ever*?

The hospital was full of men with shaved, swollen, bandaged heads, many psychologically disturbed. She prayed and prayed.

Some days Roy showed a little movement and her hopes soared….then nothing!

Then, after three weeks which seemed like years, he regained consciousness.

Alongside her delight she could hear the warning of the consultant. Would Roy include her in his life – would she ever be able to even hold his hand again? For weeks, she had sat for hours, whenever allowed, holding his hand; healing currents of love flowing through. The thought of life without him, *especially now;* she needed him – he was *her* life support. Even worse - w*ould he be permanently handicapped?*

After the hospital staff had examined him, she was allowed to sit by his bed again. She smiled at him hopefully and he spoke:

'I've been watching you sitting here. When I get out of here I'm going to marry you.'

Tears moistened her eyes, then trickled unstoppably down her face. Even the bossiness of his proposal was pure ecstasy; it made him sound back to normal and when he was more recovered she would be able to tell him that they already were married *and*.......that she was expecting his baby!

Chapter 22.

LABOUR OF LOVE!

The strong, stout man in a bowler hat huffed and wheezed his way up the steps of the Blackpool B&B and through the front doors. He banged hard on the reception bell. A small woman came scuttling through the interior doors:

'I'm sorry we're all full........Capel?' Mary was astonished to see him on the doorstep. All the Allen family and friends and friend's families had been coming up to the guest house. Indeed it was always full and had plenty of helpers, but was not a financial success as there were not many rooms left for full paying guests. However, they were all having a great time. But Capel had shown no interest in coming. He was happy with his lot and let the family get on with their adventures. His 'lot' consisted of: getting up at dawn, with the birds - an exalting time of day, never to be missed. He would take his dog a walk along to the local tip and help himself to useful things for the neighborhood. He kept all the local children's bikes mended with his bits and bobs and provided pushchairs, coffee tables, bits of everything from his old Anderson shelter, all free. He worked down the pit, then had his daily dominoes with his mates and a few pints of 'rough' (the cheaper beer as opposed to 'best') at his local; 'The old Boat.' He wasn't interested in cavorting round Blackpool. He liked a quiet life and never got in the way of his wife and family, as long as his dinner was waiting for him at home.

'Where's my missus?' he said, 'Where's Maud?'

'Come on through, Capel. They're all having lunch. You can have some with them'.

Capel was surprised at how many people he recognized in the dining room. It was almost like going home or to his local pub. Two of his young grandchildren stopped racing round the tables and ran to greet him. Maud nearly choked on her tea. Was it something serious?

'Here, let's get you some lunch then we'll go

somewhere private,' she said diplomatically. Food always soothed him and everyone had stopped to listen.

At last they were alone.

'It's got to stop, Maud,' he shook his head. 'I'm worried about that young gal. She needs help.'

'What Shirley?' Maud pulled a face. There was no love lost there and Maud had seen Shirley's arrival as an opportunity for her to join everyone and help run the guest house. She had left Shirley to do the sandwiches for work, dinners and keep house for 5 men including Capel and all the animals. She'd hoped the task would send her running off and leave her beloved Roy alone. She clearly wasn't good enough for her son.

'What's she been saying then?'

'Nothing. She never complains. You've misjudged her Maud. You've all misjudged her. She's worked like a Trojan while you lot have been cavorting up here. She's a bloody marvel. She goes to work as well and……she's not long off having a baby but she's so thin.' He shook his head, 'She looks ill - the poor kid needs help.'

Maud started to feel guilty. She was normally so good to people, but she had been sure this girl was just a floozy turning up at their house so young. Roy was tough but she knew that he was very deep and she didn't want him hurt. She had thought a bit of pressure and Shirley would run off with someone else. Sooner rather than later would be less hurtful for her son. Well she had no luck there, she had hoped maybe absence would work, with Roy away for National Service, but if anything the parting and Roy's accident had brought them even closer. Thankfully, Roy was now making a good recovery in a convalescent hospital.

'No Maud you've misjudged this one, and our Roy adores her. The letters he writes her, you've never seen anything like it.'

'Our Roy writing….*letters*….And she lets *you* read them?'

'   No,' he laughed, 'But they're easy enough

to steam open with the kettle and seal back up.' The crafty monkey always knew a lot more than he let on to everybody. Maud nodded seriously:

'We'll have a nice day on the beach and there's some brilliant amusements to show you, you'll love it and tonight we'll have a sing song....then I'll come back with you - first train in the morning.'

She explained to the others. They felt really guilty. Perhaps they had seriously misjudged Shirley. They remembered Christmas. Roy had given one of his sister's money to buy Shirley a really nice present because he didn't feel confident about shopping and choosing it himself. In the excitement she had forgotten and let the shops close, so they had wrapped up an old pair of granny-type slippers, with a checked pattern and a bobble on, that they had bought for an elderly lady. They'd been worried about the repercussion from their brother but it never came. Shirley must have kept it to herself.

Capel had a real day to remember at the seaside. He laughed till he cried in the hall of mirrors and rolled up his trousers to paddle in the sea with an ice cream *and* a candy floss. No wonder they had all stayed on longer in Blackpool. The day after tomorrow he would be back down the black pit, crawling on his hands and knees deep under the ground. But living for the moment was part of his soul, and, wow did he have a great day.

Shirley had indeed kept all the animosity to herself. Yes, she had once enjoyed dressing up and getting whistled and asked out by all the young men - but that was before she had met *him. S*he had never even come close to feeling like this about anyone. Whatever anyone said or did to her she must remain at the Allen's – until he came home. If she left they might turn him against her. He was everything to her, absolutely everything. She had worshipped him from afar as a child and now she had his deep love. A love that she had never known. She couldn't contemplate existence without him. His letters were her oxygen. Every knock on the door raised her spirits in case it was a phone call for her. On the rare occasions that he was able Roy would ring the telephone kiosk in the street. Anyone passing nearby, usually children out playing, would run to her house to tell her that she had a call. In the winter she spent many freezing hours in the phone box. She struggled on, doing her best to please. She knew that if she let out her incubated anger she wouldn't be able to restrain it and could risk being thrown out, so she suppressed it and toiled on. At first, she had quite liked having only the men and animals there, being lady of the house and they really appreciated what she did, but she started to feel so tired and ill. She should have quit work but struggled on, saving for their own home, until... she lost her babies. And now she was expecting another. Maud ... and the others couldn't let that happen again; whether the guest house needed them or not, they would return en masse.

Chapter 23.

I WILL BRING YOU FLOWERS.

Roy was going home at last. The last year had nearly killed him. After gaining consciousness, he had remained at the brain hospital. At first, he hadn't told the doctor's when he was starting to feel a lot better for fear that he would be sent straight back to the barracks; but the brain hospital was a daunting place. One night whilst lying on the bed, in his hospital room, smoking a cigarette, a tall man with a very swollen bald head and protruding eyes came into his room. The man came over to the bed, put his head by Roy's so that their faces were touching, and stared at the cigarette in Roy's mouth. Frightened, Roy handed him the lighted cigarette. The man put the whole cigarette *in* his mouth, as if to eat it, and then ran wailing out of the room.

At his next medical consultation Roy was much improved, but feared that he wasn't ready to return to the barracks. The doctor's agreed but said that he still wasn't fit to go home. Luckily they sent him to a convalescent hospital - by the sea with luxury food – venison and steak.

After a few weeks he was called for another consultancy and feared the worst as he stood before the judging panel, feeling fit. The decision was the one that he had dreamed about for over a year – they were sending him home!

Don collected him from the railway station. How glad Roy was to step out of the station and see his elder brother. The feeling was mutual. Don was so relieved to see him safe and sound. They'd not been raised to hug and show affection in public, but they beamed at one another with intense affection. Don punched Roy playfully on the arm:

'Come on Ruey, they're all waiting for you.'
'Ruey!' He was Ruey again. The last year blotted out, his old name back.

Don had had a productive few years. Married to Nancy, the daughter of one of the farmers over the nearby fields. They now had a son and their own house and were planning to buy a smallholding and have chickens and horses. Don's fetching and carrying everyone everywhere was starting to pay and he was considering his own light haulage business. Roy had missed so much, but he was only half listening. As the lorry entered the long lane that leads from the main Coventry road into the small community of Blackhorse road, Roy felt his heart pump faster, and his spirits soar, like returning from war and sighting the white cliffs of Dover. A small, mostly council house estate – home!

Shirley waited excitedly. She'd have gone with Don to fetch him. In fact she'd have walked there, had she not been so near to having another baby. But this time she was being sensible. She wasn't risking this baby for anything. And she was so worried. Would she miscarry? Would this one live? Everyone was looking after her now. Maud had got the whole community knitting for the new baby. Joyce, her sister in law had given her the most beautiful crib. It was light blue with a drawer underneath. She'd only seen cribs like it in pictures of royalty.

Would she have Roy's baby safely? Would Roy be the same old Ruey after his traumatic accident? She wished she didn't look so fat; she was enormous. How could he possibly fancy *her*?

Doubts and worries melted away as he gave her that beaming grin of his:

'How's my little Viking? Or should I say Vikings. Looks like you're having about ten of em,' he teased. Whatever he said, his eyes and his all- encompassing smile said more. They said that he clearly adored her. She felt like an elephant, but he picked her up like she was a kitten. Once again, she felt like a little child, secure and adored, protected and safe – and so happy. Only he could do that.

He wanted everybody else to disappear. Just to be with her, but of course there was everybody to consider. All his loved ones and a whole lot more who wanted to be nosey or didn't want to miss a party. And so it continued. They had looked forward to this day so much. Finally, exhausted, Shirley went to bed. Their own room now – but not quite! Shirley and the dog had got very attached to one another. Had the dog sensed her deep insecurity and need for love that she hid so well from the rest of the world? It had become very protective and, as Roy finally managed to escape from the crowd and join her, he faced a fierce, growling monster. No way was the dog going to let him into bed. It snarled savagely. It would fight to the death. He could see Shirley, asleep on the bed, just as he had dreamed of her. She was very tired due to the weight of the pregnancy and the long months of anxiety, but looked happy and so relaxed now. There was no way that dog would let him sleep with his angel tonight, without disturbing her. But there'd be other days.

He returned to the party and had a great time, winning at cards; his family were so pleased to have him back. And a friend told him about a good firm that was recruiting and paying well, but he needed to come with him first thing in the morning.

Shirley got up next morning feeling stressed. He hadn't slept with her. He wasn't even in the house.

'Ruey was the life and soul of the party last night, it's great to have him back, you should have seen how much he won at cards,' she heard someone saying. They didn't realise how much the words hurt her. After she'd waited for him – and he wasn't even here now. Shirley's two big toes started curling up and down, up and down. This always happened when she tried to keep her anger bottled; like a saucepan lid raising up and down as it is lifted by hot steam, before it boils over. But she knew she'd have to simmer. Separation, his illness, her elephant shape and tiredness. Maybe it would take a bit of time to get back to normal. But get him back she would!

She found out that he'd gone to get a job. But why hadn't he kissed her goodbye. The day seemed like a week. It was almost her bedtime when he returned. He'd worked hard. It had gone well, then he hadn't really wanted to go to the pub but wanted to make a good impression with work colleagues. He really needed this job with the baby on the way. Shirley was enormously relieved to find out that he hadn't slept with her because of the dog. Her life had changed forever. She could only sleep happily if he was there. He had become so much a part of her that she felt anxious as if a part of her was missing if he wasn't there. But she had to feel like this a lot. He was soon working ridiculously long hours, and fast asleep as soon as his head hit the pillow. Her anxiety increased as she worried about the coming birth, but now an additional worry – was her husband going off her? Well, she couldn't do much about it now. Soon the birth would be over and she was determined she'd get her figure back - and her husband.

Capel, was always there for her. He'd grown to love her like a daughter and worried about her.

'Come on me little beauty, sup this up. Guiness is good for ya,' he'd say, messing up the top of her hair with a friendly gesture. 'Don't worry your pretty head about our Roy. He's young and stupid but he's alright is our Roy. He loves you. Everything'll be alright. You'll see.' He was used to having to reassure everyone but really he was worried. Roy had always kept things to himself and was coming home ridiculously late. He didn't know of a job that kept you that long. What was he playing at? Shirley looked so sad; it was heart breaking to watch. *He'd* just have to look after her.

Shirley was getting more stressed and uncomfortable. It was a very hot August and she just couldn't get comfortable no matter how she sat. The baby wasn't due for another week or so. She decided to go a walk down the lane. Nearing the pub round the corner, she felt a sharp pain. She stood still panting. A few minutes later, another sharp pain convulsing the mass of her body. She leaned against the wall. She could see Capel's trilby hat ; She knew it was his, he always sat in the same place and his hat just showed over the writing in the pub window. She banged on the window. Someone came out.

'Can you get Capel for me,' she said. Well Capel was just having a nice relaxing game of dominoes and had downed about ten pints of 'rough' but was never one to ignore a distress signal.

He took one look at her and knew instantly what was happening.

'Your face has gone green m'dear. Don't you worry about a thing; Capel'l look after you,' he slurred. He picked her up and started to stagger with her towards his house.

'I can walk, Capel, really.'

But he wasn't listening; full of the confidence that ten pints of 'rough' inspires and likewise sapped of the ability to think clearly or coordinate his limbs. He set off. Shirley started shrieking as he nearly lolloped into a nearby ditch. Well he'd experienced many births and heard them shrieking before, so took no notice.

Her waters broke all over him and still he staggered on, a real trooper.

'Nearly there, m' dear, stay calm, nearly there; Capel'l look after you.' His journey was twice as long as normal, as he couldn't walk in a straight line, but lolloped from one side of the road to the other. Somehow he managed to get to the house and carried her, protesting and shrieking even more, upstairs to her bedroom.

'*Maud*! *Maud!*' they both called. Luckily Maud came running.

'What are you doing up here? Downstairs! It's *downstairs! We*'ve put everything ready *downstairs*!'

Capel looked at Shirley and grabbed her again. A very strong man, she had no chance of escaping as he carried her downstairs. Despite the house being overcrowded, the front room had been cordoned off and prepared especially for the birth, with a single bed and the beautiful cot and new towels. It was nearer the kitchen for hot water and so that Shirley wouldn't have to *get up the stairs*. Task finally completed Capel lolloped onto the nearest chair and was soon snoring. Maud made Shirley comfortable, then went into the street. She shouted her neighbour to:

'Fetch the midwife, quickly the baby's coming.' Then she instructed a young boy, playing football out in the street to go to the place where Roy was working and tell him his wife was having the baby. It wasn't customary to have men in the delivery room but Capel was a big man, there was no moving him yet. Likewise no one dare challenge the dog who'd snook under the bed.

It was agony for Roy as well, on arrival he had to just wait in the next room, as men were only allowed in the delivery room if they were doctors. Shirley had experienced such grief over losing the twins. It was agony being able to do nothing but wait. His dad joined him after an hour or so; he knew from experience what Roy was going through:

' Just….keep boiling the kettle son, just keep boiling the kettle…..and we'll have a drop of the hot water for tea….I've saved a drop of whisky to put in it.'

Baby 'Roy', as it had been named was a beautiful little girl. Shirley just could not believe it. Not the fact that she was a girl but that *she* had given birth to this beautiful miracle. The pain of the last few hours quickly forgotten; there is no feeling in the world as wondrous as your first child.

Capel and Maud left the happy threesome in their hypnotic state. The outside world faded away as, intoxicated with love, the proud mum and dad sat hugging and trance-like, staring at their own tiny miracle.

And this continued for ...... several weeks. It was customary for everyone to have a look at a new baby and put silver coins in its hands, but Roy was having none of that. In fact hardly anybody was allowed near in case they had germs. The couple took it in turns to stay awake at night watching the baby in case she stopped breathing. If she slept too soundly, they woke her up to make sure she was breathing. After a few days, Roy had to go and register the baby and return to work, but he still did his nightly watches....and fell out with his dad for leaning over the big bouncy pram, and Shirley's sister by refusing to let her take the baby just over the shop. This was the intensely loving Roy that Shirley had fallen in love with. She was ecstatic to have the lovely baby and to have him back, properly back. Naming the baby had been the biggest decision of their lives. No name seemed beautiful enough for their... treasure. Finally, thoughtfully Roy had announced that:

'It would be nice to name her after that hospital that I was in.'

' WALTHAM?' Shirley questioned horrified at the thought.

'No, the other one,' he laughed, 'the convalescent one - *Victoria*.'

His obvious reluctance to go back to work warmed Shirley's heart. He wanted to be with her as much as she wanted him. However, after a few weeks, her sense of security started to dissipate, as he returned home later and later, and clearly not just from work as his breath smelled of beer. Shirley didn't know what to do. She worked hard at getting her figure back and dressed up, but he hardly seemed to notice, as he came back, ate, then went to bed and to sleep as soon as his head touched the pillow. He was out of the house seven days a week, early in the morning until late at night. She tried unsuccessfully to reason with him.

'... Not now Shirl. I'm bushed.' Then her worst fears were realized; She sobbed into her pillow all night, hugging their baby as he... didn't come home.

She couldn't believe that she had loved and believed in him so completely. Had she fallen in love with a heartless liar and adulterer?

Where would she go with a baby, what could she do, how could he do this to her, *how could he do it to Victoria?*

Her tears dried up and anger started to bubble up inside her. The volcanic lava seeped from the pit of her stomach into her limbs.

It was now Saturday morning when in he walked:

'Sorry sweetheart, it was too late to come home. I fell asleep...' Smash! A bedside lamp hit the wall beside him. The volcano had erupted! He swerved to miss a bottle of perfume. Running low on ammunition and further angered by her objects missing their target, she charged at him with the poker from the fireplace. Luckily for him, his boxing and street fighting had given him lightning reactions. He grabbed the poker and threw it behind him, then with his really long, strong arms held her at arms length, so that her flailing fists and kicking legs couldn't reach him. This made her madder and her arms and legs kicked faster and more furiously, but to no avail. In fact he had a big grin on his face:

'Oh, you're really something. You're so cute when you're angry. I can explain.' He saw her face. 'Wait, I'll show you. Get you and the baby ready.'

She, did as he bade, silently. 'It had better be good,' she thought, ' or I'll never speak to him again.' They set off with their bundle in the beautiful princess pram, with lace around the bonnet. They had been so proud, so happy. How *could* he ruin it? Faithful Cinders followed, leadless at her heels. Roy looked really worried. Their journey was going towards his work.

'Well he needn't think some work project that he had been working on was a good enough excuse.' She knew he wasn't even there sometimes when he was supposed to be. She was too angry to speak to him. After walking silently for twenty five minutes they turned into Recreation Road. Well surprise, surprise this road led to Windmill road where he worked. Her anger started to boil up again. She looked at him, furiously. He looked worried to death. He *was* worried because he didn't think she'd be very pleased with what he was about to show her, especially in this mood; he'd never seen her like this.

About half way up the street, he stopped.

'Changed your mind about showing me then? Why doesn't that surprise me,' she said sarcastically.

'…We're here Shirl- this is it.' He looked at the cream semi-detached cottage on their right. She gulped. She'd have far preferred a work project. Her voice was tearful.

'… Is this where she lives?'

'I'm so sorry, Shirl I wanted it to be better than this for you. You deserve better.'… He realized what she'd said: 'Who lives? What are you on about…. Here's the keys.'

Shirley could hardly open the front door. Her hands were shaking so much. Unexpectedly, he scooped her up and carried her over the threshold.

'Now don't get mad again, it's not finished yet, I've got plans.'

She was totally speechless as he led her around.

'This is the living room. I'm putting a new fireplace in.' There was a big pile of bricks and rubble in the living room where he had smashed out the old one.

He pointed to the door in the corner: 'That's the stairs – it's got two bedrooms; one of 'em's massive - it'll hold a lot of kids.' She followed him, mystified.

'This is the kitchen.' He opened a massive fridge. 'I got it from a butcher. It doesn't work but we can store tins in it. We need a big one I'm gonna fill it with food for you. You're never gonna go hungry.' Apart from an old sink, the fridge almost filled the kitchen. To the side of the sink a large hole in the wall was covered with a board. They went through another door. He looked pleased here as he proudly explained: 'It's got an indoor toilet, Shirl, and a bath. This copper works. It boils the water lovely, I've tried it. You put this little hose on and turn this and the hot water goes into the bath.' She still hadn't spoken a word.

He was talking faster now, getting more nervous. He led her out of a side door into the back garden. It was a cross between a scrap heap and a building site. He explained: ' Me and Joyce's husband (who was a car mechanic) have bought these cars to do up. When we sell 'em we can have proper thick carpets.' Carpets- she'd never lived in a house with carpets. His mum had rugs on oil cloth and a strip down the middle of the stairs so that the hall looked presentable to visitors at the door. Her own childhood home had only the home-made hearth rug.

At the end of the garden were some broken chicken pens covered in chicken poo and a broken fence. 'I'll mend all this and I thought you might like a few banty hens. Then here we can have vegetables. Then, that bit by the mulberry bush,' he pointed to the area by the house, 'You can fill with flowers.' She looked. She no longer saw the breeze blocks and rubble and old cars... only flowers. Her own garden of....flowers. She started to cry. 'Don't cry Shirl, I'll work night and day until we get it right. These breeze blocks are for the kitchen. My mate, Fred's a builder. He'll show me how to do it and help do the roof 'n' stuff, as long as I keep the beer flowing. We've started knocking the wall down. You can have the kitchen as big as you like and keep the other room for best.' She was now sobbing. 'I know it's a mess. But I will do it. I haven't had much chance these last few months I've been doing two jobs to get it paid for.' She started to cry loudly. ' Look if you want, I'll just sell it;' he said dejectedly. 'The main reason I wanted *this* house is because it's near my work. I can come home and see you in my lunch hour and, if I run, in my afternoon break as well....and I've made sure it's near a shop and a school and a park for kids...and it's not far from your mother's. Your dad wants you to visit. He sent you these:' he picked up a box with two bedside lamps in, one with a pink rose on and one a blue. At home her dad hadn't let her have a light in the bedroom.

Shirley was now sobbing....all the tears from the years that she hadn't cried.

Finally, still crying, she spoke:

'I'm not crying because I don't *like* the house. .....I'm crying because, sniff, sniff ...I'm *so happy!*'

'Well, bloody Nora, weren't women strange', he thought.

They went back into the living room - *their* living room. There was an old table with three chairs and a crate of beer on it. He opened a bottle with his pen knife while she fetched the baby in.

'Where's mine?' she asked.

'I thought you didn't like alcohol.'

'Well, your old man's been educating me,and after today I think I need one.' He opened a few more bottles:

'We'll just have a few, then I'll get you both home,' he said.

'What do you mean, home?.... We are home.' she said dreamily and kissed him, passionately,... very passionately.

311

'There's no bed yet, I slept in the old jag outside last night.'

'Well, you'd better get cracking then, cos I'm going nowhere,' she said.

He looked pleased, then perplexed. There was no bed, no heating, no pots and pans, the list was endless. But, she looked determined. He laughed, swigged back his bottle of beer, kissed her again and ran out the door. He'd need to borrow a lorry and...!

This time, she knew he'd be back. She just couldn't move. She was in a daze; she just couldn't believe it. She sat there in her own home so happy with her baby and dog. She couldn't believe that she deserved such a marvelous man as him...all this. His words echoed around her head: ' Loads of food... a garden *full* of flowers,' things that she'd *longed* for as a child. This man could see into her very soul. He was her soul. She just sat and sat....for hours. Before she knew it she'd swigged back another bottle of beer, and another. She wasn't much used to alcohol and hadn't thought to eat all day. She started to feel a bit tipsy.

Suddenly, behind her back, she heard strange heavy breathing... then pig-like snuffling. Startled, she turned. It was coming from the open letterbox. She could see a nose, an animal's nose. She looked out of the window and saw a bulldog. It must have followed her dog. She'd forgotten that Cinders was in season. Shirley had only seen bulldogs in books and newspapers. They were associated with Churchill's British spirit of never giving up and courage in adversity. She'd thought how fierce and ugly the dogs looked. She eyed him curiously. Close up, he looked quite friendly and lovable. She returned to her bottle. Raindrops started to tap on the makeshift bathroom roof; their drumming became louder, faster... She wondered was 'Winston' still there? She peered out of her window... Well, of course he was! He was sitting there in the drizzle. He opened his mouth. Was he yawning.......no, he looked like he was laughing. Shirley laughed:

'Well, hic, here's a toast to you bulldog.' She raised her beer bottle.

She looked at the pile of broken bricks and rubble

313

where a fireplace should be; no big deal really, after surviving the Coventry blitz. Alcohol turned the words in her head into philosophical ping pong balls and she contemplated the past: Churchill's vitality had resonated via his words, reinforcing the strength of his listeners. Hitler had thrown a rope of words to rescue many of his listeners; then used the rope as a noose around their neck. Shirley contemplated the power of words - how they filled people's heads and activated them - especially empty young heads. She gazed at her baby. She would grow up with two adoring parent's, a free spirit....what words would fill her now tiny head? Shirley's happiness grew and grew until it was too much for just her own body. She decided to let some of it out with words. She raised her beer bottle to the audience that she couldn't see:

'Here's a toast to *us* bulldogs.......In fact, here's a toast...........to........

.........BULLDOGS
EVERYWHERE!'

Roy with his elder brothers; Don
and Les Allen (Left to right).

Shirley Thompson